GCSE Success

REVISION GUIDE

French

Steve Harrison

Contents

Lifestyle

Revised

The Wider World

Revised

Vocabulary and Grammar

Revised

Exam Advice

Listening and Reading

All instructions and questions in both reading and listening tests are now in English. Each test is worth 20% of the total marks, making 40% for both skills combined. At foundation tier, examiners have to set papers using the word lists printed in the specification. At higher tier, there are additional words to learn and some unfamiliar words may be used. You should be able to work out the meaning of these new words using communication strategies (see pages 86–87). Many of the questions will be multiple choice, but other tasks – such as true / false / not mentioned (in reading only), matching exercises, gap fill and answers in English – will also be used. Here are some tips for tackling these comprehension questions:

- Keep revising vocabulary as often as you can. Generally, the more words you know, the easier the tests will be.

- In listening tests, you are given 5 minutes before the CD starts to read through the questions. Use this time sensibly and make notes on the paper if necessary.

- Read the questions carefully. You would be surprised how often people misread questions. For example, in answer to the question 'Apart from football, what other sports does she like?' it is not uncommon to find candidates writing 'football' as their answer.

- Do not panic if you do not understand everything you hear and every single word you read. Working out the gist is the key skill.

- Never leave a blank space. If you are genuinely stuck, make a sensible guess.

- Make sure you form letters clearly and write legibly. If you do decide to cross out an answer, write the new answer as

near as possible to the original and make it absolutely clear what your final answer is. Always use a black pen. Your papers will be scanned and marked online.

- Look out for negative expressions, which often catch people out.

- Do not assume the first word you see or hear is the one you need for your answer. **Je ne vais plus au collège en voiture, j'y vais en bus** means the speaker now goes to school by bus and not by car.

- Recognition of tenses is important. Look at or listen to verb endings with great care.

- High frequency words such as **souvent**, **quelquefois**, **jamais**, **encore** and **sauf** can change the meaning of a sentence. **Il va au gymnase tous les jours sauf le dimanche** means that he does not go to the gym every day despite the phrase **tous les jours**, since **sauf** means 'except'.

- When revising vocabulary, try to learn words in categories so that you can see the connections between words. If there is a question about a person's favourite leisure activity, the answer could be 'reading' but the word **la lecture** (reading) may not be used at all. Terms such as **un roman** (a novel) or **un journal** (a newspaper) might be used instead.

✔ Maximise Your Marks

Many questions at A* require you to recognise emotions, so to reach this grade make sure you have revised words such as **heureux** (happy), **triste** (sad), **inquiet** (worried).

Speaking

The speaking component is worth 30% of the total marks and is tested through controlled assessments. You will have to submit marks for two pieces of speaking that you have done during your GCSE course. These will be marked by your teacher. Each assessment lasts about 4–6 minutes. You will be given a task by your teacher and you can then plan what you want to say. You are allowed to have a sheet with up to 30 or 40 words* on it to guide you as you do the task.

- Be aware that at the end of the test your teacher will ask an additional question that you will not have prepared. The answer does not need to be a long one but should contain a verb.
- Make sure you always give plenty of opinions during your talk.
- Include a variety of time frames, past, present and future, showing a good variety of tenses.

*The exact number of words depends on your exam board. Check this with your teacher.

- Take care that you avoid the temptation to pronounce the **–s** at the end of words like **dans**.
- Avoid answers that are very brief. Always try to develop what you say.
- Make your sentences longer by including connectives such as **parce que**, **qui**, **où** and **cependant**.

✓ Maximise Your Marks

To get an A* you are expected to justify your opinions. This means saying why you like or dislike something. So get into the habit of always adding **parce que** whenever you say **j'aime** or **je n'aime pas**. For example:
- **Je n'aime pas l'anglais** parce que **c'est ennuyeux et le prof est nul.**
  I don't like English because it's boring and the teacher is hopeless.

Writing

The writing component is also worth 30% of the total marks and is tested through controlled assessments. You will have to submit two pieces of writing that you have done during your GCSE course. These will be marked by the exam board. Each assessment should be between 100 and 350 words*. You will be given a task by your teacher and you can then plan what you want to write. You are allowed to have a dictionary plus a sheet with up to 30 or 40 words* on it to guide you as you do the task.

- Use a variety of tenses and give plenty of personal opinions and reasons.
- Make sure you use your dictionary to check spellings and genders. Avoid the temptation to look up new words – you can end up making errors, such as writing 'une allumette de football'. This does *not* mean a football match, since **une allumette** is a match you strike to get fire. The French for a football match is **un match de football**.

- Longer, more complex sentence always score more marks.
- Make use of adverbs, adjectives and pronouns to make your work more personal and interesting.

*The exact number of words depends on your exam board. Check this with your teacher.

✓ Maximise Your Marks

Many questions at A* require you to narrate events. This means you should make sure part of your answer is in the past tense and tells the reader about a sequence of events. So use words such as **d'abord** (first), **puis** (then), **ensuite** (afterwards), **plus tard** (later) and **enfin** (finally).

Basic Phrases and Expressions

The Alphabet

A as in **ami**
B as in **un bébé**
C as in **fiancé**
D as in **un détective**
E as in **il pleut**
F as in **efficace**
G as in **j'ai**
H as in **une vache**
I as in **midi**

J as in **j'y vais**
K as in **un coca**
L as in **belle**
M as in **j'aime**
N as in **moyenne**
O as in **un gâteau**
P as in **un canapé**
Q as in **vaincu**
R as in **Air France**

S as in **une promesse**
T as in **une tasse de** thé
U as in **quel âge as-tu?**
V as in **un vélo**
W say **double vé**
X as in **Astérix**
Y say **ee grec**
Z say **zed**

Greetings

À bientôt	See you soon
À demain	See you tomorrow
À tout à l'heure	See you very soon
Allô	Hello (on the phone)
Amitiés	Best wishes
Bien sûr	Of course
Bienvenue	Welcome
Bon anniversaire	Happy birthday
Bon appétit	Enjoy your meal
Bon voyage	Have a good journey
Bonne année	Happy New Year
Bonne chance	Good luck
Bonne idée	Good idea
Bonne nuit	Goodnight
Bonnes vacances	Have a good holiday
Bonsoir	Good evening
Bravo	Well done
Ça va?	How are you?
Excusez-moi	Excuse me
Félicitations	Congratulations
Pardon	Excuse me/Sorry
Salut	Hello/Goodbye (informal)
A ta/votre santé!	Cheers!

Useful Expressions

Je ne sais pas	I don't know
Je ne comprends pas	I don't understand
D'accord	OK (agreement)
Comment?	Pardon?
Désolé(e)	Sorry
C'est vrai	That's true
Ce n'est pas vrai	That's not true
Vraiment?	Really?
Pouvez-vous m'aider?	Can you help me?
Tout de suite	Straight away
Je veux bien	Yes, please
Non merci	No, thanks
De rien	Don't mention it
Un instant!	Wait a bit!
Attends!	Wait!
Au secours!	Help!
Au feu!	Fire!
Au voleur!	Stop, thief!
C'est sûr?	Is that definite?
Je vous en prie	Don't mention it
Où sont les toilettes?	Where are the toilets?
C'est gentil	That's kind
Quel dommage!	What a shame!
Il ne fallait pas	You shouldn't have
Oh là là!	Dear me!
Zut!	Blast!

Numbers

0	**zéro**	22	**vingt-deux**
1	**un**	23	**vingt-trois**
2	**deux**	30	**trente**
3	**trois**	31	**trente et un**
4	**quatre**	35	**trente-cinq**
5	**cinq**	40	**quarante**
6	**six**	50	**cinquante**
7	**sept**	60	**soixante**
8	**huit**	70	**soixante-dix**
9	**neuf**	71	**soixante et onze**
10	**dix**	72	**soixante-douze**
11	**onze**	73	**soixante-treize**
12	**douze**	80	**quatre-vingts**
13	**treize**	81	**quatre-vingt-un**
14	**quatorze**	82	**quatre-vingt-deux**
15	**quinze**	90	**quatre-vingt-dix**
16	**seize**	91	**quatre-vingt-onze**
17	**dix-sept**	95	**quatre-vingt-quinze**
18	**dix-huit**	99	**quatre-vingt-dix-neuf**
19	**dix-neuf**	100	**cent**
20	**vingt**	101	**cent un**
21	**vingt et un**	1000	**mille**

about 10	**une dizaine**
about 20	**une vingtaine**

first	**le premier/la première**
second	**le deuxième/la deuxième/**
	le second/la seconde
third	**le troisième/la troisième**
fourth	**le quatrième/la quatrième**

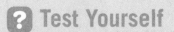

Days, Months and Dates

lundi	Monday
mardi	Tuesday
mercredi	Wednesday
jeudi	Thursday
vendredi	Friday
samedi	Saturday
dimanche	Sunday

janvier	January
février	February
mars	March
avril	April
mai	May
juin	June
juillet	July
août	August
septembre	September
octobre	October
novembre	November
décembre	December

Quelle est la date aujourd'hui?
What's today's date?

Aujourd'hui, c'est mercredi dix-huit mars.
Today is Wednesday the 18th of March.

C'est le vingt avril deux mille onze.
It's the 20th of April 2011.

Introduction

? Test Yourself

1 How would you say in French 'the 1st of January'?

2 Put these numbers in the correct order from lowest to highest:
**vingt-cinq   quarante-deux   douze   cent un
soixante-deux   soixante-douze**

★ Stretch Yourself

1 What would you say in French:
   a) to someone about to go to bed?
   b) to someone about to take an exam?
   c) to someone who has passed an exam?

Basic Phrases and Expressions

Introduction

Telling the Time

Quelle heure est-il?	What time is it?
À quelle heure?	At what time?

Il est...	It is...
midi	midday
minuit	midnight
une heure	one o'clock
trois heures	three o'clock
cinq heures cinq	five past five
six heures et quart	quarter past six
dix heures et demie	half past ten
onze heures moins vingt	twenty to eleven
midi moins le quart	quarter to twelve

du matin/soir
in the morning/evening

de l'après-midi
in the afternoon

à minuit et demi
at half past midnight

à six heures du soir
at six o'clock in the evening

à neuf heures moins vingt-cinq
at twenty-five to nine

✓ Maximise Your Marks

Remember that the French use the 24-hour clock more often than we do:
- **treize heures dix** 1.10 p.m.
- **vingt et une heures** 9 p.m.
- **seize heures trente** 4.30 p.m.
- **une heure quarante** 1.40 a.m.

Colours

C'est de quelle couleur?	What colour is it?
rouge	red
bleu	blue
vert	green
jaune	yellow
blanc/blanche	white
noir	black
gris	grey
orange	orange
brun	brown
marron	brown
rose	pink
roux/rousse	ginger (red hair)
blond	blonde
violet	purple
bleu clair	light blue
bleu foncé	dark blue

✓ Maximise Your Marks

Remember to make the colours agree if you put them with a feminine or plural noun:
- **C'est un chat noir.**
  It's a black cat.
- **C'est une souris noire.**
  It's a black mouse.
- **J'ai des chaussures noires.**
  I've got black shoes.
- **Elle a les cheveux noirs.**
  She's got black hair.

But note that when you use **clair** or **foncé**, the colour does *not* agree:
- **Elle porte une jupe bleu clair.**
  She's wearing a light blue skirt.

Being Polite

There are two words for 'you' in French: **tu** and **vous**.

You can use **tu** when speaking to a friend, a member of your family or an animal. For example:
- **Où habites-tu?** Where do you live?

If you are speaking to more than one friend, relative or animal, use **vous**. For example:
- **Où habitez-vous?** Where do you live?

You must also use **vous** if you are speaking to one person politely, such as a waiter, a shop assistant or a stranger.

There are two ways to say 'please':
- **s'il te plaît** is used for someone you address with **tu**.
- **s'il vous plaît** is the polite form.

Question Words

Quand?	When?
Que?/Qu'est-ce que?	What?
Qui?	Who?/Which?
Quel/quelle/quels/ quelles?	What?/Which?
Où?	Where?
Pourquoi?	Why?
Comment?	How?
Combien?	How many/much?
Combien de temps?	How long?

Comment can also be used when you are asking someone to describe something or someone:
- **Comment est ta maison?**
  What's your house like?

Abbreviations

CDI (centre de documentation et d'information) school library

CES (collège d'enseignement secondaire) secondary school

EPS (éducation physique et sportive) PE

HLM (habitation à loyer modéré) social housing

SAMU (Service d'aide médicale d'urgence) ambulance service

SIDA AIDS

SNCF (Société nationale des chemins de fer français) French rail

TIC (technologies de l'information et de la communication) ICT

TGV (train à grande vitesse) high-speed train

TVA (taxe sur la valeur ajoutée) VAT

VTT (vélo tout terrain) mountain bike

❓ Test Yourself

1. Which is the odd one out?
   juillet   jeudi   juin   janvier
2. Put these times into the 24-hour clock:
   Il est six heures et demie du soir.
   Il est huit heures et quart du matin.

⭐ Stretch Yourself

1. Say or write in French: 'Where is your house?'
2. Say or write in French: 'I've got a white mouse!'

Personal Information and Family

Talking About Yourself

Je m'appelle…
I am called…

Mon prénom est…et mon nom de famille est…
My first name is… and my surname is…

J'ai un frère/une sœur.
I have a brother/a sister.

Il/Elle s'appelle…
He/She is called…

J'ai deux sœurs, mais je n'ai pas de frères.
I have two sisters, but I don't have any brothers.

Je suis fils/fille unique.
I'm an only child.

Mes frères s'appellent…et…
My brothers are called…and…

J'ai quinze ans.
I'm 15.

Mon père a trente-huit ans.
My dad's 38.

✓ Maximise Your Marks

If you are asked to describe your family, try to include negatives as well.
- **J'ai une sœur mais** je n'ai pas de frères.
- **J'ai un chien mais** je n'ai pas de chat.
- **J'ai beaucoup de cousins mais** je n'ai pas de cousines.

Build Your Skills: 'Qui'

Instead of saying: **J'ai une sœur. Elle s'appelle Sophie** (I have a sister. She is called Sophie), you can use the word **qui** to link the sentences together: **J'ai une sœur** qui **s'appelle Sophie** (I've a sister who's called Sophie). Here are some more examples:
- **Mon frère,** qui **s'appelle Oscar, a seize ans.**
  My brother, who is called Oscar, is 16.
- **J'ai un chien** qui **est noir et blanc.**
  I've got a dog which is black and white.

Family Members and Pets

le bébé	baby
l'enfant	child
la famille	family
la fille	daughter/girl
le fils	son
le frère	brother
le garçon	boy
la grand-mère	grandmother
le grand-père	grandfather
les grands-parents	grandparents
l'homme	man
la maman	mum
la mère	mother
l'oncle	uncle
le papa	dad
le/la partenaire	partner
le père	father
la sœur	sister
la tante	aunt
le beau-père	step-father/father-in-law
la belle-sœur	step-sister/sister-in-law
le demi-frère	half-brother
la demi-sœur	half-sister
aîné(e)	older
cadet/cadette	younger
le cousin	male cousin
la cousine	female cousin
un jumeau	male twin
une jumelle	female twin
le neveu	nephew
la nièce	niece
le petit-fils	grandson
la petite-fille	grand-daughter
le chat	cat
le cheval	horse
le chien	dog
le cochon d'Inde	guinea pig
le lapin	rabbit
l'oiseau	bird
le poisson rouge	goldfish
la souris	mouse

Gender, Singular and Plural

French nouns are either masculine or feminine. You can usually tell by the article in front of them what gender the words are.

Le père and **le frère** are masculine, as you would expect, but so are **le chien** and **le lapin**.

La fille and **la sœur** are feminine, but so are **la famille** and **la souris**.

Le and **la** both change to **les** in the plural:
- **les frères**, **les parents**

Un chien is masculine; **une famille** is feminine.

Un and **une** both change to **des** in the plural:
- **des chiens**, **des familles**

Look out for words beginning with a vowel or a silent **h**, e.g. **l'oncle**, **l'homme**. These are, as you would expect, masculine but **l'oiseau** is less obvious. But when you see **un oiseau**, you realise that it is masculine.

To make a word plural, you usually add **–s** (but this is often silent in French):
- **un chien**, **deux chiens**
- **la fille**, **des filles**

Words ending in **–s** do not change:
- **un fils**, **deux fils**

Words ending in **–eau** often add **–x**:
- **un oiseau**, **cinq oiseaux**

Words ending in **–al** change to **–aux**:
- **un animal**, **des animaux**
- **un cheval**, **trois chevaux**

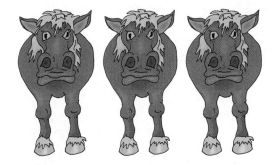

How to Say 'My', 'Your', 'His' and 'Her'

To say 'my' in French, you need to know if the word you are describing is masculine, feminine or plural, and then use **mon**, **ma** or **mes**:
- **Mon frère s'appelle Paul et ma sœur s'appelle Pauline. Mes parents sont sympas.** My brother's called Paul and my sister's called Pauline. My parents are nice.

To say 'your' in French, use **ton**, **ta** or **tes**:
- **J'adore ton père mais ta mère est pénible.** I love your dad but your mum gets on my nerves.
- **Tes cousins sont gentils.** Your cousins are nice.

Be careful with **son**, **sa** and **ses**, which can mean 'his' or 'her' depending on what you are talking about:
- **Ma tante a un chien. Son chien s'appelle Toto.** My aunt has a dog. *Her* dog's called Toto.
- **Mon oncle a une tortue. Sa tortue s'appelle Rapido.** My uncle has a tortoise. *His* tortoise is called Rapido.

Note that feminine words beginning with a vowel or silent **h** take **mon**, **ton** and **son**, e.g. **mon amie**, **son enfant**.

❓ Test Yourself

1. Which is the odd one out?
   le lapin   la souris   le chat   le hamster
2. How would you say in French: 'my mother', 'my goldfish', 'my cats'?
3. How would you say in French: 'I have two dogs, three horses and five birds.'?
4. What does this mean in English?
   Ma cousine est fille unique.

★ Stretch Yourself

1. Say or write in French: 'My friend has a sister who is five years old.'
2. Say or write in French: 'I have a cat that is black and white.'

Describing Yourself and Others

Finding Out About Other People

Comment t'appelles-tu?
What's your name?

Je m'appelle Caroline.
My name is Caroline.

Quel âge as-tu?
How old are you?

J'ai seize ans.
I'm 16.

Quelle est la date de ton anniversaire?
When's your birthday?

C'est le vingt mai.
It's the 20th of May.

Où habites-tu?
Where do you live?

J'habite à Leeds.
I live in Leeds.

De quelle couleur sont tes yeux?
What colour are your eyes?

J'ai les yeux verts.
I've got green eyes.

Comment sont tes cheveux?
What's your hair like?

J'ai les cheveux courts.
I've got short hair.

Tu as des frères et des sœurs?
Do you have any brothers and sisters?

J'ai un frère et deux sœurs.
I've got one brother and two sisters.

Comment s'appelle ton frère?
What is your brother's name?

Il s'appelle Arthur.
He's called Arthur.

Quel âge a-t-il?
How old is he?

Il a dix ans.
He's 10.

Comment est-il?
What does he look like?

Il est petit avec les cheveux blonds.
He's small with blond hair.

Quelle est la date de son anniversaire?
When is his birthday?

C'est le deux septembre.
It's the 2nd of September.

Two Key Verbs: 'Avoir' and 'Être'

Avoir (to have)	Être (to be)
J'ai I have	**Je suis** I am
Tu as You have	**Tu es** You are
Il/Elle a He/She has	**Il/Elle est** He/She is
Nous avons We have	**Nous sommes** We are
Vous avez You have	**Vous êtes** You are
Ils/Elles ont They have	**Ils/Elles sont** They are

When giving ages, you use **avoir**, not **être** as you might expect. For example:

- **Quel âge as-tu?**
  How old are you?
- **J'ai seize ans, mais j'ai presque dix-sept ans.**
  I'm 16, but I'm nearly 17.
- **Ils ont quinze ans tous les deux.**
  They're both 15.

Using 'Avoir' and 'Être'

Je suis petit(e) et mince.
I'm small and slim.

Il est grand. Elle est grande et maigre.
He is tall. She is tall and thin.

Ils sont de taille moyenne.
They are of medium height.

Ma sœur est belle, mais mon frère est moche.
My sister is beautiful, but my brother is ugly.

J'ai les cheveux bruns / châtains et frisés.
I have brown, curly hair.

Elle a les cheveux blonds et raides.
She has blond, straight hair.

Il a les cheveux roux et les yeux verts.
He has ginger hair and green eyes.

Mon frère a les yeux noisette.
My brother has hazel eyes.

Ma sœur a les yeux gris.
My sister has grey eyes.

Mon amie a les cheveux mi-longs.
My friend has medium-length hair.

✓ Maximise Your Marks

Although **avoir** and **être** are important verbs, they can be overused. Try to use alternatives if you can to vary your language. So instead of saying **il est beau** (he is good-looking), you can say **il me semble beau** (he seems good-looking to me – i.e. I think he's good-looking).

You could also use an expression which contains **avoir** but sounds more impressive. For example, **elle est sympa** (she's nice) can be changed to **elle a l'air sympa** (she looks nice).

Comparing People

You can make comparisons by using one of the following three words with an adjective:

plus   more
moins   less
aussi   as

After the adjective you use **que**:
* **Mon frère est plus sportif que ma soeur.**
  My brother is more sporty than my sister.
* **Ma mère est plus généreuse que mon père.**
  My mother is more generous than my father.
* **Mon ami est moins bête que mon frère.**
  My friend is less stupid than my brother.
* **Ma sœur est aussi intelligente que moi.**
  My sister is as clever as me.

The French for 'better' is **meilleur(e)**:
* **Mon ami est un meilleur chanteur que moi.**
  My friend is a better singer than me.

But with a verb, use **mieux** for 'better':
* **Mon ami chante mieux que moi.**
  My friend sings better than me.

To say 'the best', use **le meilleur, la meilleure** or **les meilleurs (les meilleures)**:
* **La cuisine française est la meilleure du monde.**
  French cooking is the best in the world.

Pire is the French for 'worse' / 'worst':
* **Il chante pire que moi.**
  He sings worse than I do.

Home Life

❓ Test Yourself

How would you say these in French?
1. My mother is 37 and has long hair.
2. My sister is small and slim.

What do these mean in English?
3. **Ma cousine a les yeux noisette.**
4. **Mon père est grand et maigre.**

⭐ Stretch Yourself

1. Say or write in French: 'My brother is not as intelligent as your sister.'
2. Say or write in French: 'I'm taller than my friend but I'm smaller than my brother.'

Character and Personality

Describing Someone's Personality

sympa	nice, friendly	**animé(e)**	lively
casse-pieds	a nuisance	**compréhensif/**	understanding
gentil/gentille	kind	**compréhensive**	
impatient(e)	impatient	**fier/fière**	proud
généreux/généreuse	generous	**fou/folle**	mad
amusant(e)	funny	**optimiste**	optimistic
méchant(e)	naughty	**poli(e)**	polite
drôle	witty	**tranquille**	calm/quiet
patient(e)	patient	**fâché(e)**	angry
timide	shy	**jaloux/jalouse**	jealous
bête	stupid	**déprimé(e)**	depressed
égoïste	selfish	**impoli(e)**	rude
intelligent(e)	clever	**méchant(e)**	nasty
ennuyeux/ennuyeuse	boring	**pessimiste**	pessimistic
plein(e) de vie	full of life	**triste**	sad
sérieux/sérieuse	serious		
sévère	strict		
bavard(e)	talkative/chatty		
travailleur/travailleuse	hard-working		
maladroit(e)	clumsy		
vif/vive	lively		
amoureux/amoureuse	in love		
jeune	young		
heureux/heureuse	happy		
malheureux/malheureuse	unhappy		
marrant(e)	funny		
aimable	nice/pleasant/kind		
amical(e)	friendly		

Mon frère est travailleur et ma sœur est sérieuse.
My brother is hard-working and my sister
is serious.

Ma tante est généreuse et elle est pleine de vie.
My aunt is generous and she's full of life.

Ma copine est timide et elle n'est pas bavarde.
My friend is shy and she is not talkative.

Adjectives

Adjectives are very useful words for describing someone's appearance or personality. Remember, in French, the ending of the adjective depends on whether the person you are describing is masculine or feminine, or whether you are describing one person or more. For example:

- **Mon père est grand.**   My father is tall.

- **Ma mère est grande.**   My mother is tall.

- **Mes parents sont grands.** My parents are tall.

Adjectives ending in **–x** change to **–se** in the feminine, for example:

- **Mon frère est paresseux et ma sœur est paresseuse, elle aussi.**
  My brother is lazy and my sister is lazy too.

! Boost Your Memory

Revise characteristics by looking at photos in a magazine and using French adjectives to describe the people in them. For example:
Il est beau. Elle est bizarre.

Intensifiers

If you are using adjectives to describe your family, try to include intensifiers as well. These make what you say or write more interesting. Three useful intensifiers are **très** (very), **assez** (fairly) and **trop** (too). To remind you of these words, think of TAT (**très**, **assez**, **trop**). For example:

- **Mon ami est très poli, mais de temps en temps il est assez ennuyeux.** My friend is very polite, but sometimes he's fairly boring.

💡 Boost Your Memory

To help you revise, think of some celebrities and decide what they are like using intensifiers. For example: **Johnny Depp est très beau**, **Brad Pitt est assez beau**, etc.

'–er' Verbs

Many verbs in French are **–er** verbs. The advantage of these verbs is that they follow the same pattern. Make sure you know all the correct endings.

The verb **travailler** (to work) is an **–er** verb. Here is the present tense of **travailler** in full:

Je travaille	I work, am working
Tu travailles	You work, are working
Il/Elle travaille	He/She works, is working
Nous travaillons	We work, are working
Vous travaillez	You work, are working
Ils/Elles travaillent	They work, are working

Elle travaille dur.
She works hard.

Ils travaillent ensemble.
They work together.

Build Your Skills: Exceptions and Irregular Forms

Some adjectives are irregular. Watch out for these three adjectives: **vieux** (old), **beau** (beautiful) and **nouveau** (new). They have a special masculine form when the noun begins with a vowel or a silent **h**. For example:

un beau **garçon**	a good-looking boy
une belle **fille**	a beautiful/ good-looking girl
un bel **enfant**	a beautiful child
un nouveau **partenaire**	a new partner
une nouvelle **femme**	a new wife
un nouvel **ami**	a new friend
le Nouvel **An**	New Year
un vieux **monsieur**	an old gentleman
une vieille **dame**	an old lady
un vieil **homme**	an old man

Some **–er** verbs also have spelling changes. Take the verbs **appeler** (to call) and **acheter** (to buy):

J'appelle	**J'achète**
Tu appelles	**Tu achètes**
Il/Elle appelle	**Il/Elle achète**
Nous appelons	**Nous achetons**
Vous appelez	**Vous achetez**
Ils/Elles appellent	**Ils/Elles achètent**

Nous appelons **le magasin.**
We're calling the shop.

Tu achètes **une nouvelle voiture?**
Are you buying a new car?

Home Life

❓ Test Yourself

How would you say these in French?
1. My mother is serious but she is nice.
2. My sister is boring and lazy.

What do these mean in English?
3. **Je suis gentil et amusant.**
4. **Mes parents sont sévères et impatients.**

⭐ Stretch Yourself

1. Say or write in French: 'The old lady is buying a new car.'
2. Say or write in French: 'I'm calling my uncle.'

Relationships

What Is the Relationship?

le mari	husband
la femme	wife
amoureux/amoureuse	in love
le bonheur	happiness
célibataire	single
un copain	male friend
une copine	female friend
divorcé(e)	divorced
mort(e)	dead
né(e)	born
la naissance	birth
un petit ami	boyfriend
une petite amie	girlfriend
séparé(e)	separated
seul(e)	alone/lonely
veuf/veuve	widower/widow

Mon ami est compréhensif et aimable.
My friend is understanding and nice.

Ma petite amie est jolie et marrante et je peux compter sur elle.
My girlfriend is pretty and funny and I can rely on her.

Ma meilleure copine a beaucoup d'humour.
My best friend has a very good sense of humour.

Mes parents critiquent mes vêtements et ils n'apprécient pas mes amis.
My parents criticise my clothes and they don't appreciate my friends.

Je connais mon frère. Il est trop impatient. Il parle avant de réfléchir.
I know my brother. He's too impatient. He speaks before thinking.

💡 Boost Your Memory

Take a TV family and draw a family tree, describing the correct relationships. For example, in Bart Simpson's family tree, **Homer est son père**, etc.

'–re' Verbs

The verb **rendre** ('to make' + adjective) is an **–re** verb. Here is the present tense in full:

Je rends	I make, am making
Tu rends	You make, are making
Il/Elle rend	He/She makes, is making
Nous rendons	We make, are making
Vous rendez	You make, are making
Ils/Elles rendent	They make, are making

Other **–re** verbs are **répondre** (to reply/answer), **vendre** (to sell) and **entendre** (to hear).

Elle me rend heureux.
She makes me happy.

Je rends mes parents tristes.
I make my parents sad.

Build Your Skills: Reflexive Verbs

Some verbs are reflexive verbs: you need to use a pronoun when you use the verb. Here is the verb **se disputer** (to argue) with the correct pronouns in full:

- **Je me dispute avec mon frère.**
  I argue with my brother.
- **Est-ce que tu te disputes avec tes parents?**
  Do you argue with your parents?
- **Elle se dispute tout le temps avec ses copines.**
  She's always arguing with her friends.
- **Nous nous disputons souvent.** We often argue.
- **Vous vous disputez avec vos sœurs?**
  Do you argue with your sisters?
- **Ils se disputent au sujet de l'argent.**
  They argue about money.

Other useful reflexives are **s'entendre avec** (to get on with), **se confier à** (to confide in) and **se méfier de** (to be mistrustful of):

- **Elle s'entend bien avec sa sœur aînée.**
  She gets on well with her older sister.
- **Nous nous entendons à merveille.**
  We get on really well.
- **Je me dispute avec mes parents.**
  I argue with my parents.
- **Elles se confient à ma sœur.**
  They confide in my sister.

Emphatic Pronouns

After words such as **avec** (with), **pour** (for) and **sans** (without), you need to use a special set of pronouns:

moi me	nous us
toi you (singular, friendly)	vous you (polite singular, plural)
lui him	eux them (m.)
elle her	elles them (f.)

- **Je m'entends avec eux.**
  I get on with them.
- **Il est toujours là pour moi.**
  He's always there for me.
- **Je ne peux pas vivre sans toi.**
  I can't live without you.
- **Ils se disputent avec nous.**
  They argue with us.

These pronouns are also used for emphasis, so they are known as emphatic pronouns:

- **Toi, tu n'aimes pas les gens tristes.**
  You don't like sad people (you don't).
- **Moi, je suis travailleuse, mais mon frère est paresseux, lui.** (Me) I'm hard-working but my brother's lazy (he is).

✓ Maximise Your Marks

Always try to give reasons when you have made a statement or given an opinion.

- **Je n'aime pas le petit ami de ma sœur parce qu'il est arrogant.** I don't like my sister's boyfriend because he's arrogant.
- **Il s'entend bien avec son copain parce qu'il est amusant et gentil.** He gets on well with his friend because he's funny and kind.

❓ Test Yourself

How would you say these in French?
1. My parents don't like my clothes.
2. My boyfriend makes me sad.

What do these mean in English?
3. **Tu peux compter sur moi.**
4. **Ma sœur est célibataire et elle se dispute souvent avec moi.**

★ Stretch Yourself

1. Say or write in French: 'I never confide in him because we don't get on.'
2. Say or write in French: 'You argue all the time, you two.'

Relationships in the Future

Home Life

The Verbs 'Aller' and 'Vouloir'

Aller (to go) is an important verb. It is also often used to talk about future plans when it is followed by the infinitive of another verb, e.g. **Je vais acheter une grosse voiture** (I'm going to buy a big car). The verb **vouloir** (to want) is also useful for talking about what you want to happen, e.g. **Je veux me marier** (I want to get married).

Je vais	I go, am going
Tu vas	You go, are going
Il/Elle va	He/She goes, is going
Nous allons	We go, are going
Vous allez	You go, are going
Ils/Elles vont	They go, are going
Je veux	I want
Tu veux	You want
Il/Elle veut	He/She wants
Nous voulons	We want
Vous voulez	You want
Ils/Elles veulent	They want

Talking About Your Future Relationships

Je ne vais jamais me marier.
I'm never going to get married.

Je vais me marier à l'âge de 30 ans.
I'm going to get married when I'm 30.

Je veux rester célibataire.
I want to stay single.

Tu vas avoir des enfants?
Are you going to have children?

Il veut avoir deux enfants – une fille et un garçon.
He wants to have two children – a girl and a boy.

Elle veut avoir des jumeaux/jumelles.
She wants to have twins.

Laure va épouser son partenaire idéal.
Laure's going to marry her ideal partner.

Useful Words for Talking About Future Plans

les enfants	children
épouser	to marry
féliciter	to congratulate
fêter	to celebrate
les fiançailles	engagement
heureux/heureuse	happy
le mariage	marriage
se marier avec…	to get married to…
la naissance	birth
les noces	wedding
le partenaire idéal	ideal partner (male)
la partenaire idéale	ideal partner (female)
le plaisir	pleasure
riche	rich
une alliance	a wedding ring
l'amour	love
attendre	to wait
une bague	a ring
célèbre	famous
les adolescents	teenagers
les adultes	adults
les jeunes	young people
une famille nombreuse	a large family
les noces d'argent	silver wedding (anniversary)
un bébé	baby
enceinte	pregnant
un heureux événement	a happy event
une fête familiale	a family celebration
le troisième âge	older people
les rapports	relationships
une mère célibataire	a single mother
une famille monoparentale	a single-parent family
le PACS	civil partnership
les vieux	old people

Build Your Skills: Varying Your Language – Future Plans

Using the verb **aller** or **vouloir** with the infinitive is a good way of expressing future intentions but there are other alternatives which can improve the style and complexity of what you say or write. The following are all used with the infinitive to convey future plans:

Je voudrais	I'd/I would like
Je pense	I'm thinking
Je rêve de	I dream of
J'ai l'intention de	I intend to
Je pourrais	I might/could
J'espère	I hope, am hoping

Je voudrais **avoir deux enfants.**
I'd like to have two children.

J'ai l'intention d**'aller à l'université avant de me marier.**
I intend to go to university before I get married.

À l'avenir je pourrais **devenir célèbre.**
In the future, I might become famous.

J'espère **être riche.**
I hope to be rich.

'–ir' Verbs

A lot of French verbs end in **–ir**. The present tense of many (but not all) verbs ending in **–ir** is formed like the verb **finir** (to finish) as follows:

Je finis	I finish, am finishing
Tu finis	You finish, are finishing
Il/Elle finit	He/She finishes, is finishing
Nous finissons	We finish, are finishing
Vous finissez	You finish, are finishing
Ils/Elles finissent	They finish, are finishing

Other **–ir** verbs that have the same endings include **choisir** (to choose), **remplir** (to fill), **rougir** (to blush), **réfléchir** (to reflect/think) and **saisir** (to seize). For example:

- **Les enfants finissent leurs devoirs.**
  The children are finishing their homework.

- **La fille rougit quand elle parle de son petit ami.**
  The girl blushes when she talks about her boyfriend.

✓ Maximise Your Marks

In answering questions at GCSE most of the time you will be talking about yourself. To make your answers more interesting and to show off your knowledge of a range of structures, try occasionally to mention someone else. For example:

- **Mon ami veut se marier plus tard dans la vie mais moi je veux rester célibataire.** My friend wants to get married in later life but I want to stay single.

- **Je voudrais aller à l'université mais ma copine a l'intention de voyager.**
  I'd like to go to university but my friend intends to travel.

❓ Test Yourself

How would you say these in French?
1. She wants to be rich and famous.
2. I'm going to marry an actor.
3. What does this mean in English? **Je veux parler à ton frère mais je rougis facilement.**
4. Which of these verbs is not a regular **–ir** verb?
   saisir   finir   rougir   remplir   sortir   choisir

⭐ Stretch Yourself

1. Say or write in French: 'My friend intends to have a big family.'

2. Say or write in French: 'I hope to go to university because I might become a teacher.'

House and Home

Describing Your Home

Dans ma maison, il y a trois pièces au rez-de-chaussée: le salon, la cuisine et la salle à manger.
In my house there are three rooms downstairs: the lounge, the kitchen and the dining room.

Au premier étage, il y a quatre chambres, les WC et une salle de bains.
Upstairs there are four bedrooms, the toilet and a bathroom.

Il y a la chambre de mes parents, ma chambre, la chambre de mon frère et une chambre d'amis.
There's my parents' room, my room, my brother's room and a spare room.

Il y a un petit jardin devant la maison et un grand jardin derrière.
There's a small garden in front of the house and a large garden behind.

Le garage est à côté de la maison.
The garage is next to the house.

chez moi	at my house
le bureau	study
la cave	cellar
une chambre	bedroom
la cuisine	kitchen
le grenier	attic/loft
une pièce	room
le salon	lounge
la salle à manger	dining room
la salle de séjour/le salon	living room
la salle de bains	bathroom
les WC	toilet
la véranda	conservatory
le garage	garage
le jardin	garden
un arbre	tree
une fleur	flower
le gazon	grass
la pelouse	lawn
une cabane/un abri	shed
une maison individuelle	a detached house
une maison jumelée	a semi-detached house
un appartement	a flat
une ferme	a farm

ⓘ Boost Your Memory

Revise the rooms of the house by writing an estate agent's advert to sell your own home. Use adjectives to make it more interesting:
Il y a un grand salon, il y a une belle cuisine moderne, il y a un vaste jardin...

The Verb 'Faire'

Faire is a useful verb, meaning 'to do' or 'to make'. Note the irregular **vous** and **ils/elles** forms in the present tense:

Je fais
Tu fais
Il/Elle fait
Nous faisons
Vous faites
Ils/Elles font

Faire is used in a lot of expressions that are to do with jobs around the house. For example:

faire la cuisine	to do the cooking
faire les courses	to go shopping
faire le jardinage	to do the gardening
faire la lessive	to do the washing
faire le lit	to make the bed
faire le ménage	to do the housework
faire le repassage	to do the ironing
faire la vaisselle	to do the washing-up

The Verb 'Faire' (cont.)

Qu'est-ce que tu fais pour aider à la maison?
What do you do to help at home?

Mon père fait les courses.
My father does the shopping.

Mon frère fait le repassage.
My brother does the ironing.

Mes parents font le jardinage.
My parents do the gardening.

J'aime faire la cuisine, mais je déteste faire mon lit.
I like doing the cooking, but I hate making my bed.

Other chores include:

laver	to wash
débarrasser la table	to clear the table
mettre la table	to set the table
passer l'aspirateur	to do the vacuuming
promener le chien	to walk the dog
sortir la poubelle	to put the bin out
ranger	to tidy
nettoyer	to clean

Je mets la table tous les jours et ma sœur fait la vaisselle.
I set the table every day and my sister washes up.

J'aime promener le chien mais j'ai horreur de sortir la poubelle.
I like walking the dog but I can't stand putting out the bin.

✓ Maximise Your Marks

When talking about what you do at home, make your answer more interesting by including adverbs of time to say how often you do it. Use **rarement** (rarely), **souvent** (often), **quelquefois** (sometimes) and **de temps en temps** (from time to time).
For example:
- **Je fais souvent la vaisselle, mais je range rarement ma chambre.**
  I often do the washing-up, but I rarely tidy my room.

Build Your Skills: Using 'Qui', 'Que', 'Dont'

Qui is used to say 'who' or 'which' when there is a verb immediately after it. It can be used for people or objects. For example:
- **J'ai ma propre chambre qui est très grande.**
  I have my own room, which is very large.
- **C'est mon père qui fait la cuisine chez nous.**
  It's my dad who does the cooking at home.

Que is used to say 'which' or 'whom' when there is a pronoun immediately after it. For example:
- **J'ai une petite chambre que j'adore.**
  I have a small bedroom, which I love.
- **Ma mère est une personne que je respecte beaucoup.** My mother is a person whom I respect greatly.

Dont is used to say 'whose'. For example:
- **C'est le professeur dont la maison est jolie.**
  It's the teacher whose house is pretty.
- **Voici la famille dont la maison est grande.**
  There's the family whose house is big.

❓ Test Yourself

How would you say these in French?
1. Downstairs, there is a large lounge and a kitchen.
2. I like vacuuming but I rarely do the ironing.

What do these mean in English?
3. **Mes parents travaillent souvent dans le jardin.**
4. **La chambre de mon frère est souvent en désordre.**

★ Stretch Yourself

1. Say or write in French: 'My friend, who is lazy, has a sister whose bedroom is very clean.'

2. Say or write in French: 'She has a brother whose wife is German.'

Talking About Your House

Saying Where Your House Is

Ma maison se trouve...	My house is situated...
au centre-ville	in the town centre
en banlieue	in the suburbs
à la campagne	in the country
au bord de la mer	at the seaside
à la montagne	in the mountains
près de la ville	near town
dans un village	in a village
loin de la mer	a long way from the sea

Ma maison est près de la gare; c'est pratique.
My house is near the station; it's convenient/handy.

Ma maison n'est pas près du centre-ville et c'est loin des magasins. Ce n'est pas très commode.
My house is not near the town centre and it's a long way from the shops. It's not very convenient/handy.

Saying What Is In Your House

une armoire	a wardrobe
une bibliothèque	a bookcase
un canapé	a sofa
le chauffage central	central heating
la cuisinière	cooker
la douche	shower
un escalier	stairs
une étagère	a shelf
un évier	a sink
un fauteuil	armchair
une fenêtre	window
un (four à) micro-ondes	microwave (oven)
un frigo	fridge
un lavabo	basin
un lave-vaisselle	dishwasher
une machine à laver	washing machine
les meubles	furniture
un miroir	mirror
une moquette	carpet
un ordinateur	computer
un placard	cupboard
le plancher	floor
le plafond	ceiling
une porte	door
un réveil	alarm clock
un tapis	carpet/rug

Dans ma chambre, il y a un lit, une armoire et une chaise.
In my room, there's a bed, a wardrobe and a chair.

Les murs sont blancs et les rideaux bleus.
The walls are white and the curtains blue.

Je partage ma chambre avec mon petit frère.
I share my room with my little brother.

J'ai ma propre chambre.
I have my own room.

Saying Where Things Are

The following words are called prepositions.
They are used to describe where something is.

dans	in
sur	on
sous	under
devant	in front of
derrière	behind
entre	between
à côté de	next to
en face de	opposite
au coin de	in the corner of
à gauche de	to the left of

Il y a deux fauteuils dans le salon.
There are two armchairs in the lounge.

La cuisine est à côté de la salle à manger.
The kitchen is next to the dining room.

Le jardin est devant la maison.
The garden is in front of the house.

Le lit est entre la fenêtre et la porte.
The bed is between the window and the door.

Le chat est sous le lit. The cat is under the bed.

✓ Maximise Your Marks

Be careful if the word after **à côté de** or **en face de** is masculine. Be careful *not* to say 'de le'; instead, use **du**. For example:

- **La petite table est à côté du lit.**
  The little table is next to the bed.
- **Ma maison est en face du garage.**
  My house is opposite the garage.
- **Au coin du salon, nous avons une lampe.**
  In the corner of the lounge we have a lamp.

Build Your Skills: Your Routine At Home

À quelle heure est-ce que tu te lèves?
What time do you get up?

Je me réveille à sept heures du matin.
I wake up at seven o'clock in the morning.

Je me lève tout de suite.
I get up straightaway.

Je me douche dans la salle de bains et je me brosse les dents.
I have a shower in the bathroom and I brush my teeth.

Je m'habille dans ma chambre.
I get dressed in my room.

Je prends le petit déjeuner dans la cuisine et je quitte la maison à huit heures vingt.
I have breakfast in the kitchen and I leave the house at 8.20.

Je rentre vers quatre heures.
I come home at about four (o'clock).

Je me lave les mains et je prends le dîner.
I wash my hands and have my evening meal.

Le week-end, je fais la grasse matinée.
At the weekend I have a lie-in.

À quelle heure est-ce que tu te couches?
What time do you go to bed?

Je me couche à dix heures et demie.
I go to bed at 10.30.

? Test Yourself

How would you say these in French?
1. In my room there is a large bed and a blue wardrobe.
2. The garden is behind the house, which is opposite the shop.

What do these mean in English?
3. **Ma maison est près des magasins.**
4. **Dans le salon il y a un canapé et deux fauteuils confortables.**

★ Stretch Yourself

1. Say or write in French: 'I never get up before 10 o'clock at the weekend because I like a lie-in.'
2. Say or write in French: 'I have a shower and then I get dressed.'

Home Life

23

Describing Your Local Area

What Is There In Your Area?

Au centre-ville, il y a...	In the town centre, there is...
une banque	a bank
beaucoup de circulation	a lot of traffic
une bibliothèque	a library
un centre commercial	a shopping centre
un centre sportif	a sports centre
un château	a castle
une église	a church
des embouteillages	traffic jams
une gare routière	a bus station
un hôtel de ville	a town hall
un marché	a market
un musée	a museum
un office du tourisme	a tourist information office
une piscine	a swimming pool
une zone piétonne	a pedestrian zone

Describing Where You Live

Ma ville se trouve...	My town is (situated)...
dans le nord/le sud	in the north/south
dans l'est/l'ouest	in the east/west
au centre	in the centre
de l'Angleterre	of England
de la France	of France

C'est...	It's...
une ville industrielle	an industrial town
une ville touristique	a tourist town
une ville commerciale	a commercial town
une ville historique	an historical town

The Verbs 'Pouvoir' and 'Devoir'

The verb **pouvoir** means 'to be able' ('can'). It is very useful when you want to talk about what there is to do in your area. Here is the present tense in full:

Je peux	I'm able, I can
Tu peux	You're able, you can
Il/Elle peut	He/She is able, he/she can
Nous pouvons	We're able, we can
Vous pouvez	You're able, you can
Ils/Elles peuvent	They're able, they can

On peut visiter des monuments historiques.
You can visit historical monuments.

On peut faire du shopping.
One can go shopping.

The verb **devoir** means 'to have to' ('must'). Here is the present tense in full:

Je dois	I must, I have to
Tu dois	You must, you have to
Il/Elle doit	He/She must, he/she has to
Nous devons	We must, we have to
Vous devez	You must, you have to
Ils/Elles doivent	They must, they have to

Au centre-ville tu dois visiter le musée.
In the town centre you must visit the museum.

Les touristes doivent goûter la cuisine locale.
Tourists must try the local food.

Town or Country?

À la campagne, il n'y a pas de transports en commun et il est difficile de faire du shopping. Mais l'air est pur et les paysages sont jolis. C'est tranquille et calme. On peut y voir des fermes avec des animaux.

In the country, there is no public transport and it is hard to go shopping. But the air is fresh and the scenery is pretty. It is peaceful and calm. You can see farms with animals.

Town or Country? (cont.)

En ville, il y a beaucoup de distractions et de magasins. La ville est toujours animée. Il y a toujours quelque chose à faire. Mais, aux heures d'affluence, c'est bruyant car il y a trop de voitures qui polluent l'air.

In town, there is a lot of entertainment and shops. The town is always lively. There is always something to do. But, at rush hour, it is noisy because there are too many cars, which pollute the air.

Build Your Skills: The Imperfect Tense

The imperfect tense is used to talk about what *used to* happen in the past. So you could use it to say what your area used to be like.

First, you need to know the **nous** form of the present tense:
nous avons, nous travaillons, nous prenons, etc.

Now take off the **–ons** ending and add the following endings:
–ais, –ais, –ait, –ions, –iez, –aient.

Je travaillais	I used to work
Tu travaillais	You used to work
Il/Elle travaillait	He/She used to work
Nous travaillions	We used to work
Vous travailliez	You used to work
Ils/Elles travaillaient	They used to work

The only exception is **être**, which takes the same endings but uses **ét–** as the stem:

J'étais	I was, used to be
Tu étais	You were, used to be
Il/Elle était	He/She was, used to be
Nous étions	We were, used to be
Vous étiez	You were, used to be
Ils/Elles étaient	They were, used to be

Il y a cent ans, ma ville était **industrielle, et il y av**ait **beaucoup d'usines.**
One hundred years ago, my town used to be industrial and there used to be a lot of factories.

The imperfect is also often used for descriptions in the past tense. For example:
- **L'homme av**ait **une longue barbe et il port**ait **un costume noir.** The man had a long beard and he was wearing a black suit.

It is also used to say what you *were doing*:
- **Qu'est-ce que tu fais**ais? What were you doing?
- **Je regard**ais **la télé.** I was watching TV.

✓ Maximise Your Marks

When talking about your likes or dislikes, add a phrase in the imperfect tense to make what you say more complex and more interesting.

- **J'aime le football.** J'aimais **le hockey mais maintenant je préfère le football.**
  I like football. I used to like hockey but now I prefer football.

⚡ Boost Your Memory

To revise the imperfect tense talk about what you were like when you were 7 years old: **Je regardais** *Teletubbies*, **je mangeais beaucoup de bonbons, je chantais,** etc.

❓ Test Yourself

How would you say these in French?
1. In my town there is a large shopping centre
2. You must visit the old castle.

What do these mean in English?
3. **J'adore aller à la campagne parce que j'aime la nature.**
4. **Il y a trente ans, la ville était plus calme et moins polluée.**

⭐ Stretch Yourself

1. Give the imperfect (**je** form) of the following verbs:
   finir dormir dire boire
2. Say or write in French: 'The town used to have lots of shops and the centre was busy.'

Practice Questions

 Complete these exam-style questions to test your skills and understanding. Check your answers on page 91. You may wish to answer these questions on a separate piece of paper.

Reading

1 Choose one of the following adjectives to describe each of the people listed below:
   généreuse sévère ennuyeux gentil paresseux

   a) Je m'entends bien avec mon grand-père car il est sympa et agréable.

   .... (1)

   b) Mon frère ne travaille pas à l'école et il ne fait jamais ses devoirs.

   .... (1)

   c) Ma grand-mère me donne beaucoup d'argent de poche et elle m'achète des vêtements.

   .... (1)

   d) Mon père est très strict et il ne me permet pas de sortir avec mes amis.

   .... (1)

2 In the passage below, Arthur talks about his town. Read the passage and answer the questions that follow in English.

> Albi se trouve dans le sud-ouest de la France près de Toulouse. On peut visiter les monuments, faire des promenades à la campagne et faire du shopping.
>
> En ville, il y a toujours quelque chose à faire. Je n'aime pas la campagne. Je préfère la ville parce que la campagne est trop calme et il n'y a pas beaucoup à faire. Les transports en commun ne sont pas fréquents. Quand elle était petite, ma mère habitait dans une ferme à la campagne et elle dit que c'était très ennuyeux pour les jeunes.
>
> À l'avenir je voudrais habiter dans un grand appartement à Londres, parce que je voudrais perfectionner mon anglais.

   a) Where exactly is Albi?

   .... (1)

   b) What can you do there?

   .... (3)

   c) What does Arthur say about the countryside?

   .... (1)

   d) What is his mother's opinion of the countryside and why does she say this?

   .... (2)

   e) Where does Arthur want to live in the future and why?

   .... (1)

Speaking

3 Prepare a full response in French to each of the points below.

a) Describe your family.

....

b) Describe your house.

....

c) Say what there is to do in your local area.

....

d) Give your opinion of the area where you live.

....

e) Say whether you prefer the town or the countryside and give reasons.

....

f) Say where you would like to live in the future and say why.

.... (10)

Writing

4 Imagine that you are applying to take part in a French reality TV show. You need to answer the following points in as much detail as you can.

- Your looks, personality and interests
- Your family and friends and how you get on with other people
- Where you live and what you think about the area you live in
- Your ambitions for the future

....

....

....

....

....

....

.... (15)

How well did you do?

| 1–12 | Try again | 13–22 | Getting there | 23–31 | Good work | 32–37 | Excellent! |

School and School Subjects

School and Work

School Subjects

l'allemand	German	la géographie	geography
l'anglais	English	l'histoire	history
l'art dramatique	drama	l'informatique/TIC	ICT
la biologie	biology	l'instruction civique	citizenship
la chimie	chemistry	les maths	maths
le dessin	art	la musique	music
l'éducation physique	PE	la physique	physics
l'EPS (l'éducation physique et sportive)	PE	la religion	RE
		la technologie	technology
l'espagnol	Spanish	les sciences	science
le français	French	les travaux manuels	craft subjects

Giving Your Opinion

Use these adjectives to give positive opinions:

super/génial	great
intéressant	interesting
facile	easy
amusant	funny/enjoyable
utile	useful
le prof est sympa	the teacher's nice
je suis fort(e) en…	I'm good at…

Use these adjectives to give negative opinions:

nul	dreadful
ennuyeux/barbant	boring
difficile	hard/difficult
affreux/affreuse	awful
inutile	useless
le prof est sévère	the teacher's strict
je suis faible en…	I'm not very good at…

J'aime l'histoire parce que c'est amusant et le prof est sympa. I like history because it's fun and the teacher's nice.

Je n'aime pas l'anglais parce que c'est difficile et le prof est ennuyeux. I don't like English because it's hard and the teacher's boring.

Je ne suis pas très fort(e) en dessin. I'm not very good at art.

Je suis faible en musique. I'm weak at music.

Je suis fort(e) en maths. I'm good at maths.

Describing Your School

Mon collège s'appelle le Collège Baudelaire. Il y a environ neuf cents élèves. My school is called Collège Baudelaire. There are about 900 pupils.

Les bâtiments sont assez vieux. Il y a un gymnase et une bibliothèque, mais il n'y a pas de piscine. The buildings are quite old. There is a gym and a library, but there is no swimming pool.

Les cours commencent à huit heures et demie et ils finissent à quatre heures et demie. Lessons start at 8.30 and finish at 4.30.

Je suis en troisième. I am in year 10.

la sixième	year 7
la cinquième	year 8
la quatrième	year 9
la troisième	year 10
la seconde	year 11
la première	year 12
la terminale	year 13

Useful School Vocabulary

une école	school
un collège	11–15 school
un lycée	15–18 school
une école primaire	primary school
une école maternelle	a nursery
un bulletin	school report
un/une élève	a pupil
un emploi du temps	timetable
une épreuve	test
les notes	marks/results
les études	studies
passer un examen	to take an exam
réussir à/échouer à un examen	to pass/fail an exam
la pause-déjeuner	lunch break
la récréation	break
le trimestre	term
les grandes vacances	the long/summer holidays
l'appel	register
une gomme	rubber
un cahier	exercise book
un livre	book
un manuel	textbook
une règle	ruler
le règlement	school rules
un stylo	pen
un tableau noir/blanc	a black/white board
un atelier	workshop
un centre sportif	sports centre
une cantine	canteen
un laboratoire	lab
une salle de classe	classroom
une cour	playground

✓ Maximise Your Marks

The word **mais** (but) is a useful connective but there are other ways of expressing the same idea. This will add complexity to your work – an important element in achieving the top grades. For example:

- **J'aime l'anglais mais je déteste le dessin.** I like English but I hate art.
- **J'aime l'anglais. Cependant je déteste le dessin.** I like English. However, I hate art.
- **J'aime l'anglais, tandis que tu ne l'aimes pas.** I like English, whereas you don't like it.

Build Your Skills: Pronouns

When you are asked your opinion of your subjects, you can make your answer sound more interesting and natural by using pronouns:

- **Le** – as well as meaning 'the' (masculine) – is a pronoun meaning 'him' or 'it'.
- **La** – as well as meaning 'the' (feminine) – is a pronoun meaning 'her' or 'it'.
- **Les** – as well as meaning 'the' (plural) – is a pronoun meaning 'them'.

J'aime le dessin. Je le trouve intéressant.
I like art. I find it interesting.

J'adore l'histoire. Je la trouve amusante.
I love history. I find it enjoyable.

Je n'aime pas les langues.
Je les trouve difficiles.
I don't like languages.
I find them hard.

❓ Test Yourself

How would you say these in French?
1. I'm good at French but I'm not good at English.
2. The buildings are quite modern.

What do these mean in English?
3. **J'adore les maths parce que le prof est gentil.**
4. **Je n'aime pas la musique parce que le prof est sévère.**

⭐ Stretch Yourself

1. Say or write in French: 'I hate my teacher, I find him boring and he doesn't notice me.'
2. Say or write in French: 'We like history because we find it useful.'

School Rules and Uniform

School Rules

Il faut...	You must...
Il est permis de...	You're allowed to...
travailler dur	work hard
faire attention en classe	pay attention in class
être attentif/attentive en classe	be attentive in class
écouter les autres	listen to others
respecter les autres	respect others
faire les devoirs	do homework
porter un uniforme	wear a uniform
être poli	be polite

Il ne faut pas...	You must not...
Il est interdit de/d'...	It is forbidden to...
parler en classe	talk in class
porter des bijoux	wear jewellery
mettre du maquillage	wear make-up
se battre	fight
fumer	smoke
laisser tomber des papiers	drop litter
être insolent	be insolent

💡 Boost Your Memory

A good way to revise rules and uniform is to imagine some very unlikely rules or an odd-looking uniform. For example: **il faut parler en classe; il est permis de manger du chewing-gum; je veux porter une chemise verte avec un pantalon rose.**

Other Useful Verbs

apprendre	to learn
décrire	to describe
dessiner	to draw
dire	to say
écouter	to listen
écrire	to write
enseigner	to teach
épeler	to spell
étudier	to study
faire attention	to pay attention
faire les devoirs	to do homework
gagner	to win
lire	to read
obéir	to obey
parler	to speak
perdre	to lose
porter	to wear
poser une question	to ask a question
punir	to punish
quitter	to leave
répondre	to answer

Talking About the Rules

Il ne faut pas manger en classe.
You must not eat in class.

Il n'est pas permis de sortir de l'école sans permission.
It is not allowed to leave school without permission.

On ne supporte pas la violence.
Violence is not tolerated.

Il est strictement interdit de fumer.
It is strictly forbidden to smoke.

Les portables ne sont pas permis.
Mobile phones are not allowed.

Il est interdit d'écrire des graffitis.
It is forbidden to write graffiti.

Il faut être à l'heure./Il ne faut pas être en retard.
You must be on time./You must not be late.

School Uniform

l'uniforme scolaire	school uniform
les chaussettes	socks
les chaussures	shoes
les baskets	trainers
le collant	tights
le pantalon	trousers
la jupe	skirt
la chemise	shirt
le chemisier	blouse
le pullover	jumper
le blazer	blazer
la cravate	tie

Comment est ton uniforme?
What's your uniform like?

Je porte une jupe noire, des chaussettes blanches, un chemisier blanc, un pull vert et un blazer vert. I wear a black skirt, white socks, a white blouse, a green jumper and a green blazer.

Je porte un pantalon gris, des chaussures noires, une chemise blanche et une cravate rouge. Le blazer est bleu marine. I wear grey trousers, black shoes, a white shirt and a red tie. The blazer is navy blue.

Je suis pour l'uniforme car on ne voit pas de différences entre les riches et les pauvres et c'est bon pour la discipline. I'm in favour of a uniform because you can't see the difference between rich and poor and it's good for discipline.

Je suis contre. On a le droit d'exprimer son individualité. I'm against. We have the right to express our individuality.

Build Your Skills: Using 'Depuis'

If you want to say how long you *have been doing* something for in French, you use the word depuis (which also means 'since'). You must use the present tense of the verb. For example:

- **Je** joue **au tennis** depuis **cinq ans.** I've been playing tennis for five years.
- **J'**étudie **le français** depuis **la sixième.** I've been studying French since year 7.

If you have stopped doing something, you use **pendant** and the perfect tense:

- **J'**ai étudié **l'espagnol** pendant **six mois.** I studied Spanish for six months (and then stopped).

The Verb 'Prendre'

The verb **prendre** (to take) is an irregular verb. It is not an **–re** verb like **rendre**, **vendre** or **descendre**, so take care when you use it.

Here is the present tense in full:

Je prends	I take, am taking
Tu prends	You take, are taking
Il/Elle prend	He/She takes, is taking
Nous prenons	We take, are taking
Vous prenez	You take, are taking
Ils/Elles prennent	They take, are taking

The verbs **comprendre** (to understand) and **apprendre** (to learn) are formed in the same way:

- **Je ne** comprends **pas la question.**
  I don't understand the question.

? Test Yourself

How would you say these in French?
1. You must work hard and be attentive in class.
2. I am in favour of school uniform because it is practical.

What do these mean in English?
3. **Je suis contre l'uniforme parce que je n'aime pas la couleur.**
4. **J'apprends l'espagnol et c'est facile.**

★ Stretch Yourself

1. Say or write in French: 'At primary school I didn't wear a uniform but I've been wearing a tie for three years at my secondary school.'

2. Say or write in French: 'I played tennis for three years but now I don't like it.'

School Life

Positive and Negative Aspects of School

Je reçois de bonnes notes qui sont essentielles pour aller à l'université.
I get good marks which are essential to go to university.

Les profs nous aident beaucoup et ils nous donnent de bons conseils.
The teachers help us a lot and give us good advice.

Ma moyenne en maths est très bonne – 16 sur 20.
My average mark in maths is very good – 16 out of 20.

Je vais passer le bac l'année prochaine.
I'm going to sit A-levels next year.

Il y a un grand choix d'activités extra-scolaires.
There is a big choice of extra-curricular activities.

Je n'ai pas le temps de faire des activités extra-scolaires.
I don't have time to do extra-curricular activities.

On travaille tout le temps et on n'a pas de temps pour les loisirs.
We work all the time and we don't have time for leisure activities.

Certains profs ne s'intéressent pas aux élèves.
Some teachers aren't interested in the pupils.

Les profs ne nous écoutent pas et ils nous donnent trop de devoirs. C'est stressant.
The teachers don't listen to us and they give us too much homework. It's stressful.

Ma moyenne en maths n'est pas très bonne – seulement 9 sur 20.
My average mark in maths is not very good – only 9 out of 20.

Dans ma classe, certains élèves parlent trop et n'écoutent pas le prof.
In my class, some pupils talk too much and don't listen to the teacher.

Il y a beaucoup d'intimidation de la part des élèves plus âgés.
There is a lot of bullying by older pupils.

Pressures at School

Je veux devenir apprenti mais c'est difficile de trouver un apprentissage.
I want to become an apprentice but it is difficult to find an apprenticeship.

Le baccalauréat est un examen difficile.
The baccalaureat (equivalent of A-levels) is a difficult exam.

Au conseil de classe je crois que mes profs vont me proposer un redoublement.
At the meeting of class teachers I think my teachers are going to suggest I repeat the year.

Pour moi il faut plus de formation professionnelle.
I think we need more vocational training.

Mon bulletin n'est pas brillant. Mes parents me mettent sous trop de pression.
My report is not brilliant. My parents put too much pressure on me.

Dans mon collège, certains élèves sont violents et ils ne respectent pas les profs.
In my school, some pupils are violent and they do not respect the teachers.

Pronouns

Here are the direct pronouns:

me (m')	me
te (t')	you
le (l')	him/it
la (l')	her/it
nous	us
vous	you
les	them

Direct pronouns go in front of the verb.
For example:

- **Les profs ne nous comprennent pas.**
  The teachers do not understand us.
- **Le dessin? Je le déteste.**
  Art? I hate it.
- **Mon amie m'aide beaucoup.**
  My friend helps me a lot.

💡 Boost Your Memory

Try revising the pronouns by chanting them to yourself, for example in the style of an American army chant – **me**, **te**, **le**, **la**, **nous**, **vous**, **les** (repeat).

Build Your Skills: Indirect Pronouns

Here are the indirect pronouns:

me (m')	to me, for me
te (t')	to you, for you
lui	to him/her, for him/her
nous	to us, for us
vous	to you, for you
leur	to them, for them

Indirect pronouns also go in front of the verb. They are used with verbs that need an indirect object, like **donner** (to give), **dire** (to say/tell) and **parler** (to talk to). They are used to say something is done 'to' or 'for' someone.
For example:

- **Le professeur leur donne trop de devoirs.**
  The teacher gives them too much homework.
  (The teacher gives too much homework 'to' them.)
- **Il lui dit son secret.**
  He's telling him/her his secret.
  (He's telling his secret 'to' him/her.)
- **Il ne lui parle jamais.**
  He never speaks to him/her.

✓ Maximise Your Marks

As an alternative to **parce que**, you can use **pour** (for) followed by the infinitive to give a reason for doing something. For example:

- **Je veux aller à l'université pour étudier le français.** I want to go to university (in order) to study French.
- **Elle veut faire un stage pour devenir mécanicienne.** She wants to do a course (in order) to become a mechanic.

❓ Test Yourself

What do these mean in English?
1. **Mes parents ne me comprennent pas. Je les trouve trop stricts.**
2. **Dans mon collège, les activités extra-scolaires sont excellentes.**

How do you say these in French?
3. My friend talks too much in class.
4. We work all the time.

⭐ Stretch Yourself

1. Say or write in French: 'I told him to do his homework but he doesn't listen to me.'

2. Say or write in French: 'I like my teachers. I often talk to them.'

Part-time Work and Pocket Money

School and Work

Weekend Jobs

J'ai un petit job.
I have a part-time job.

Le samedi, je travaille dans un café. Je gagne cinq livres de l'heure.
On Saturdays, I work in a café. I earn £5 an hour.

Je commence à dix heures et demie et je finis vers quatre/seize heures.
I start at 10.30 and finish at about 4.

Je sers les clients et j'aide dans la cuisine. J'obtiens quelquefois des pourboires.
I serve the customers and I help in the kitchen. I sometimes get tips.

De temps en temps je fais du babysitting pour mes voisins. Je garde leur fils. Je reçois dix livres.
Sometimes I do babysitting for my neighbours. I look after their son. I receive £10.

Je livre des journaux. C'est assez bien payé mais c'est fatigant.
I deliver newspapers. It's quite well paid, but it's tiring.

Je travaille pour mes parents dans leur bureau. Je prépare le thé et je réponds au téléphone.
I work for my parents in their office. I make the tea and answer the phone.

The Verbs 'Recevoir' and 'Servir'

The verb **recevoir** (to receive) is irregular. Here is the present tense in full:

Je reçois	I receive, am receiving
Tu reçois	You receive, are receiving
Il/Elle reçoit	He/She receives, is receiving
Nous recevons	We receive, are receiving
Vous recevez	You receive, are receiving
Ils/Elles reçoivent	They receive, are receiving

Servir (to serve) belongs to a small group of irregular verbs which follow the same pattern. Here is the present tense of **servir** in full:

Je sers	I serve, am serving
Tu sers	You serve, are serving
Il/Elle sert	He/She serves, is serving
Nous servons	We serve, are serving
Vous servez	You serve, are serving
Ils/Elles servent	They serve, are serving

Other irregular verbs in this group include **dormir** (to sleep), **sortir** (to go out), **partir** (to set off), **sentir** (to smell/feel) and **mentir** (to tell lies).

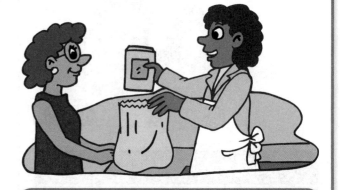

✔ Maximise Your Marks

Here are some more useful connectives to link your sentences together: **à cause de** (because of), **grâce à** (thanks to), **malgré** (in spite of), **puisque** (since) and **dès que** (as soon as).

Je dois travailler puisque je veux acheter un vélo.
I must work, since I want to buy a bike.

Grâce à sa formation, on lui a offert un poste.
Thanks to his training, they offered him a job.

Il est difficile de trouver un travail à cause de la crise économique.
It's hard for me to find a job because of the economic crisis.

Pocket Money

Avec mon argent de poche, j'achète...	With my pocket money, I buy...
de quoi manger	things to eat
des vêtements	clothes
des CD	CDs
des magazines	magazines
du maquillage	make-up

Je veux économiser de l'argent pour...	I want to save money to...
partir en vacances	go on holiday
m'offrir un vélo	treat myself to a bike

acheter...	buy...
un ordinateur	a computer
des bijoux	jewellery
des jeux-vidéo	computer games
du matériel scolaire	school materials
des cadeaux	presents

Mes parents me donnent de l'argent. Je reçois dix livres par semaine.
My parents give me money. I receive £10 a week.

Je dois aider à la maison pour avoir de l'argent.
I have to help in the house to get money.

Build Your Skills: Using Two Verbs Together

When you want to use two verbs together in the same phrase, there are three possibilities:

1. Some verbs are followed by the infinitive of the second verb, for example:
   - **Je veux trouver un petit job.**
     I want to find a part-time job.

   As well as **vouloir**, other verbs that are followed by an infinitive include **aimer** (to like), **devoir** (to have to) and **pouvoir** (to be able to). For example:
   - **Je n'aime pas servir les clients.**
     I don't like serving customers.

2. Some verbs are followed by **à** and then the infinitive, for example:
   - **Je commence à travailler à huit heures.**
     I start working at eight o'clock.

   As well as **commencer**, other verbs that are followed by **à** and then the infinitive include **encourager** (to encourage), **continuer** (to continue) and **aider** (to help). For example:
   - **J'aide le patron à préparer les sandwichs.**
     I help the boss to prepare sandwiches.

3. Some verbs are followed by **de** and then the infinitive, for example:
   - **J'essaie de gagner de l'argent pour acheter une voiture.**
     I'm trying to earn some money to buy a car.

   As well as **essayer**, other verbs that are followed by **de** and then the infinitive include **décider** (to decide), **finir** (to finish) and **arrêter** (to stop). For example:
   - **Je vais arrêter de livrer des journaux.**
     I'm going to stop delivering newspapers.

❓ Test Yourself

What do these mean in English?
1. **Je travaille dix heures par semaine.**
2. **Il n'aime pas garder son petit frère.**

How do you say these in French?
3. I earn £5 an hour.
4. She wants to find a job.

⭐ Stretch Yourself

1. Say or write in French: 'He continues to work and refuses to stop.'
2. Say or write in French: 'I help my sister to deliver the newspapers.'

Work Experience

What You Did During Work Experience

L'année dernière, j'ai fait un stage pratique.
Last year, I did some work experience.

J'ai travaillé dans une école/une banque/un magasin/un bureau.
I worked in a school/bank/shop/office.

J'ai commencé à neuf heures et j'ai fini à cinq heures et demie.
I started at 9 and I finished at 5.30.

Pendant mon stage, j'ai travaillé sur ordinateur, j'ai répondu au téléphone et j'ai photocopié des documents.
During my work experience, I worked on a computer, answered the phone and photocopied documents.

J'y ai voyagé en autobus.	I travelled there by bus.
J'ai aidé dans le bureau.	I helped in the office.
J'ai préparé le thé.	I made the tea.
J'ai servi les clients.	I served the customers.

The Perfect Tense

The perfect tense is used in French to describe events that have already happened and have a clear time limit (i.e. something that happened once and is over and done with).

To form most verbs in the perfect tense you need to use the correct form of the present tense of **avoir** followed by what is known as the past participle of the verb.

For regular **–er** verbs, you form the past participle by removing the **–er** and changing the ending to **–é**:

J'ai mangé	I ate, have eaten
Tu as parlé	You spoke, have spoken
Il/Elle a travaillé	He/She worked, has worked
Nous avons acheté	We bought, have bought
Vous avez gagné	You earned/won, have earned/won
Ils/Elles ont aidé	They helped, have helped

For irregular verbs you need to learn the past participle separately. Here is the perfect tense of **voir** in full:

J'ai vu	I saw, have seen
Tu as vu	You saw, have seen
Il/Elle a vu	He/She saw, has seen
Nous avons vu	We saw, have seen
Vous avez vu	You saw, have seen
Ils/Elles ont vu	They saw, have seen

J'ai fait la vaisselle et j'ai nettoyé les tables.
I did the washing-up and cleaned the tables.

Au déjeuner, j'ai mangé un croque-monsieur et j'ai bu du café.
For lunch I ate a toasted sandwich and drank coffee.

J'ai reçu trente livres et les clients m'ont donné des pourboires.
I received £30 and the guests/customers gave me tips.

Here are some common irregular past participles:
boire to drink	➡	**bu** drank
prendre to take	➡	**pris** taken
faire to do/make	➡	**fait** did

To make a perfect tense negative, put the negative **ne...pas** around **avoir**. For example:
- **Je n'ai pas dormi.**   I didn't sleep.
- **Ils n'ont pas bu.**   They didn't drink.

💡 Boost Your Memory

Using the past tense is so important in speaking and writing that you should learn off by heart about 10 perfect tense expressions that can be used in most contexts, for example **j'ai mangé**, **j'ai visité**, **j'ai vu**, **j'ai fait** and so on.

Saying What You Thought of Your Work Experience

The best way to do this is to use the imperfect tense:

Dans l'ensemble, le stage était...	Overall, my work experience was...
intéressant	interesting
amusant	enjoyable/funny
utile	useful
fatigant	tiring
ennuyeux	boring
une perte de temps	a waste of time
inutile	useless

Mes collègues étaient...	My colleagues were...
sympas	nice
agréables	pleasant
travailleurs	hard-working
gentils	kind
impolis	impolite/rude

Le patron était...	The boss was...
compréhensif	understanding
aimable	helpful
efficace	efficient
paresseux	lazy

✓ Maximise Your Marks

It is always impressive if you can use two different tenses in the same sentence. For example (past and present):

- **À cause de mon stage, j'ai décidé que je ne veux pas travailler dans une banque plus tard dans la vie.** Because of my experience, I have decided I do not want to work in a bank in later life.

Build Your Skills: Pronouns and the Perfect Tense

If you are forming a sentence using direct and indirect pronouns (e.g. 'me', 'you', 'him'), the pronoun goes in front of **avoir**. For example:

- **Le patron m'a donné dix livres.**
  The boss gave me £10.

- **Je leur ai parlé pendant la journée.**
  I spoke to them during the day.

A further complication is that if the pronoun is a direct one and is feminine or plural, it makes the past participle agree. Normally you must not change the past participle of a verb which takes **avoir**:

- **Voici les documents. Je les ai photocopiés pour vous.**
  Here are the documents. I've photocopied them for you.

- **J'ai acheté des fleurs et je les ai offertes à mon patron.**
  I bought some flowers and gave them to my boss.

- **La secrétaire est gentille. Je l'ai vue hier.**
  The secretary is nice. I saw her yesterday.

❓ Test Yourself

What do these mean in English?
1. **J'ai travaillé dans un grand bureau.**
2. **J'ai trouvé le travail fatigant et ennuyeux.**

How do you say these in French?
3. I served the customers – they were very nice.
4. I don't want to work in a shop in the future.

★ Stretch Yourself

1. Say or write in French: 'My boss talked to me after lunch.'

2. Say or write in French: 'The tables are not dirty. I cleaned them yesterday.'

Future Employment Plans

Jobs

un agent de police	police officer
un boucher	butcher
un boulanger	baker
un caissier/une caissière	cashier
un chauffeur	driver
un coiffeur/une coiffeuse	hairdresser
un dentiste	dentist
un directeur/une directrice	headteacher/manager
un(e) employé(e)	employee
un épicier	grocer
une mère au foyer	housewife
un homme au foyer	house husband
un facteur	postman
un fermier/une fermière	farmer
un garçon/un serveur	waiter
une serveuse	waitress
une hôtesse de l'air	air hostess
un infirmier/une infirmière	nurse
un(e) informaticien(ne)	computer analyst
un ingénieur	engineer
un(e) mécanicien(ne)	mechanic
un médecin/un docteur	doctor
un(e) dentiste	dentist
un professeur	teacher
une secrétaire	secretary
un vendeur/une vendeuse	shop assistant
un vétérinaire	vet

When talking about jobs in French, do *not* use
un or **une** before the name of the job.
For example:

- **Il est infirmier.**
  He's a nurse.
- **Elle va devenir mécanicienne.**
  She's going to become a mechanic.

Pros and Cons of Different Jobs

Je veux devenir mécanicien parce que j'adore les voitures.
I want to be a mechanic because I love cars.

Je ne veux pas devenir professeur parce que je n'aime pas les enfants.
I don't want to become a teacher because I don't like children.

Je rêve de devenir vétérinaire car les droits des animaux sont importants pour moi.
I dream of becoming a vet because animal rights are important to me.

Je veux devenir médecin pour aider les autres.
I want to become a doctor to help other people.

Pour les médecins, les heures de travail sont trop longues. C'est difficile et fatigant.
For doctors the hours are too long. It's hard and tiring.

Cependant, le salaire est très bon.
However, the pay is good.

Je veux travailler dans une ferme parce que j'aime être en plein air et je ne veux pas être enfermé dans un bureau.
I want to work on a farm because I like being in the open air and I don't want to be shut in an office.

J'aime ce travail parce qu'il me donne l'occasion de voyager.
I like this job because it gives me the chance to travel.

J'adore le contact humain/les contacts humains.
I love dealing with the public.

The Future Tense

In order to form the future tense, with most verbs (e.g. **travailler**, 'to work') you take the infinitive and add the following endings:

Je travaillerai	I'll work
Tu travailleras	You'll work
Il/Elle travaillera	He/She will work
Nous travaillerons	We'll work
Vous travaillerez	You'll work
Ils/Elles travailleront	They'll work

Note that these endings happen to be those of the present tense of **avoir**.

If the infinitive of the verb ends in **–e**, take this off before adding the future ending. For example:

Boire	➡	**Je boir**ai
Vendre	➡	**Tu vendr**as
Prendre	➡	**Il prendr**a

✓ Maximise Your Marks

Remember, there are ways of avoiding the future tense. For example, you can make use of future indicators such as **je vais, je voudrais, je veux** followed by the infinitive.

To spot the future, look out for expressions like **l'année prochaine** (next year), **la semaine prochaine** (next week), **à l'avenir** (in the future), **dans deux mois** (in two months).

Build Your Skills: Using the Future Tense with 'Quand'

Be careful with sentences containing **quand** (when). For example:

• Quand je serai **plus grande,** je serai **vétérinaire.**
  When I am older I'll be a vet.

Note that in French the future is used all the way through the sentence.

Dès que (as soon as) works in the same way. For example:

• Dès q'elle aura **dix-huit ans,** elle apprendra **à conduire.**
  As soon as she is 18, she'll learn to drive.

Some verbs are irregular in the future tense. You will need to learn these separately:

Être	➡	**Je serai** (I'll be)
Avoir	➡	**J'aurai** (I'll have)
Aller	➡	**J'irai** (I'll go)
Faire	➡	**Je ferai** (I'll do/make)
Voir	➡	**Je verrai** (I'll see)
Venir	➡	**Je viendrai** (I'll come)
Devenir	➡	**Je deviendrai** (I'll become)
Recevoir	➡	**Je recevrai** (I'll receive)
Pouvoir	➡	**Je pourrai** (I'll be able to)
Devoir	➡	**Je devrai** (I'll have to)
Vouloir	➡	**Je voudrai** (I'll like)
Savoir	➡	**Je saurai** (I'll know)
Tenir	➡	**Je tiendrai** (I'll hold)
Obtenir	➡	**J'obtiendrai** (I'll obtain)

Il deviendra fermier.
He'll become a farmer.

Il aura un bon emploi.
He'll have a good job.

◉ Boost Your Memory

Revise the future tense by writing some horoscopes for your friends: **Tu auras de bonnes nouvelles, tu voyageras, tu seras triste**, etc.

❓ Test Yourself

What do these mean in English?
1. **Je veux devenir ingénieur plus tard dans la vie.**
2. **Il ira à l'université.**

How do you say these in French?
3. Next year, I want to leave school.
4. They'll work in an office.

★ Stretch Yourself

1. Say or write in French: 'When I get married, I'll work abroad.'

2. Say or write in French: 'When I leave school, I'll find a job.'

Practice Questions

 Complete these exam-style questions to test your skills and understanding. Check your answers on page 92. You may wish to answer these questions on a separate piece of paper.

Reading

1 Read these definitions and decide what the school subject is.

A **C'est une langue. On la parle en Grande-Bretagne et aux États-Unis.**

.... (1)

B **On fait des calculs donc une calculatrice est utile pour faire cette matière.**

.... (1)

C **On fait des expériences dans le laboratoire.**

.... (1)

D **On joue d'un instrument ou on chante.**

.... (1)

E **On fait des activités physiques.**

.... (1)

F **On travaille sur des ordinateurs.**

.... (1)

G **On apprend les dates des grands événements du passé.**

.... (1)

H **On étudie les grands artistes et on fait des peintures.**

.... (1)

2 Read the passages by Carole, Flora, Églantine and Abdul below and answer the questions that follow.

J'aime bien mon école. J'ai beaucoup de copains et on s'amuse bien ensemble. Mais la cantine est trop petite et on n'a pas assez d'ordinateurs.   Carole

Je déteste l'ambiance dans mon collège. C'est très stressant. Pour les profs, seulement les devoirs sont importants. On travaille trop et on n'a pas assez de temps pour sortir avec des amis. Je ne peux pas avoir de loisirs le week-end à cause de mon travail scolaire.   Flora

L'école est très importante parce qu'il faut réussir à ses examens pour trouver un bon travail. Mais il est souvent très difficile de bien travailler en classe parce que beaucoup d'élèves n'écoutent pas le prof. Ils bavardent ou ils font des bêtises.   Églantine

À mon école, les professeurs ne sont pas très sympas. Ils ne s'intéressent pas vraiment aux élèves et ils ne nous écoutent pas. Je ne m'entends pas très bien avec eux. La vie scolaire est stressante, je trouve.   Abdul

a) Who doesn't think the teachers are very nice? .... (1)

b) Who would like better facilities at school? .... (1)

c) Who complains about other pupils' bad behaviour? .... (1)

d) Who wants to do well in exams? .... (1)

e) Who doesn't like the atmosphere in the school? .... (1)

f) Who finds school stressful? .... (1)

g) Who has a good time with friends at school? .... (1)

h) Who doesn't have enough time to do leisure activities? .... (1)

Speaking

3 Imagine you are at a new school. Prepare a response so that you can talk about each of the following in French.

a) Describe the school as it is now.

....

b) Say what subjects you like and dislike, and explain why.

....

c) Talk about your attitude to school rules, uniform and what new buildings you would like.

.... (10)

Writing

4 You are writing about your ideal job. Write about each of the following in French.
- What job you would like to do in the future and why
- What you need to do in order to get your ideal job
- Where you would like to work and why

....

....

....

....

....

....

.... (15)

How well did you do?

| 1–13 | Try again | 14–24 | Getting there | 25–33 | Good work | 34–41 | Excellent! |

Leisure Activities

Spare-time Activities

Quels sont tes loisirs?	What are your hobbies?	**Je vais au cinéma**	I go to the cinema
Que fais-tu quand tu as du temps libre?	What do you do in your free time?	**Je sors**	I go out
		Je vais en boîte	I go clubbing
		Je vais au théâtre	I go to the theatre
		Je vais à la pêche	I go fishing
		Je surfe sur Internet	I surf the net
		Je joue aux jeux-vidéo	I play computer games
		Je lis	I read
		Je regarde la télé	I watch TV
		Je joue du piano	I play the piano
		Je joue de la guitare	I play the guitar
		Je chante	I sing
		J'écoute de la musique	I listen to music

The Perfect Tense with 'Etre'

Most verbs form the perfect tense using the verb **avoir** followed by the past participle. However, a small number of common verbs use **être** instead of **avoir**. Here is the verb **aller** (to go) in the perfect tense:

Je suis allé/allée	I went
Tu es allé/allée	You went
Il est allé	He went
Elle est allée	She went
Nous sommes allés/allées	We went
Vous êtes allé/allés/allée/allées	You went
Ils sont allés	They went
Elles sont allées	They went

The following verbs form the perfect tense using **être** in the same way:

sortir (to go out)	➡	**sorti**
rester (to stay)	➡	**resté**
arriver (to arrive)	➡	**arrivé**
partir (to leave)	➡	**parti**
entrer (to enter)	➡	**entré**
monter (to go up)	➡	**monté**
descendre (to go down)	➡	**descendu**
venir (to come)	➡	**venu**
naître (to be born)	➡	**né**
mourir (to die)	➡	**mort**
tomber (to fall)	➡	**tombé**

retourner (to return)	➡	**retourné**
rentrer (to come home)	➡	**rentré**
devenir (to become)	➡	**devenu**

As with verbs that take **avoir**, negatives are formed by wrapping **ne...pas** around the correct form of **être**. For example:

- **Je ne suis pas allé au concert samedi dernier.**
  I didn't go to the concert last Saturday.

The past participle has a masculine and a feminine form. The past participle has to agree with the gender and number of the subject (**je**, **vous**, **il**, **elle**, people's names, etc.). For example:

- **Emma est allée au cinéma, mais ses frères sont allés au théâtre.**
  Emma went to the cinema, but her brothers went to the theatre.

⚠ Boost Your Memory

There are a couple of ways to remember which verbs take **être** in the perfect tense.

Most of the verbs can be put into opposing pairs: for example, **arriver** and **partir**.

Or you can use the name Mrs D van der Tramp to remind you (Mrs = **m**onter, **r**ester, **s**ortir; van = **v**enir, **a**ller, **n**aître, etc.).

Lifestyle

42

Going to the Cinema

un film d'amour	a romance film
un film à suspense	a thriller
un polar	a detective film
un western	a western
un film d'horreur	a horror film
un film d'épouvante	a scary film
une comédie	a comedy
une comédie musicale	a musical
un drame	a drama
un film historique	a historical film
un film de science-fiction	a science fiction film
un dessin animé	a cartoon/an animation

Je préfère les films comiques parce que j'aime bien rire avec mes amis. Je n'aime pas tellement les films de science-fiction, je les trouve barbants et sans intérêt.

I prefer comic films because I like a good laugh with my friends. I don't like science-fiction films very much, I find them boring and uninteresting.

Récemment, j'ai vu un excellent film français qui s'appelle *Les choristes*.

Recently I saw an excellent French film called *The Choir*.

Il s'agit d'un groupe d'élèves difficiles dans un internat dans les années 40. Un surveillant décide de créer une chorale. La musique transforme la vie de ses élèves.

It's about a group of difficult pupils in a boarding school in the 1940s. A supervisor decides to start a choir. Music transforms the lives of his pupils.

C'est un film touchant et amusant.

It's a touching and funny film.

Build Your Skills: The Verb 'Venir'

Not only is **venir** (to come) one of the irregular verbs that takes **être** in the perfect tense, it is also irregular in the present tense. Here is the present tense in full:

Je viens	I come, am coming
Tu viens	You come, are coming
Il/Elle vient	He/She comes, is coming
Nous venons	We come, are coming
Vous venez	You come, are coming
Ils/Elles viennent	They come, are coming

Note that all verbs which are compounds of **venir** – for example, **devenir** (to become), **revenir** (to come back) – are formed in the same way.

How to Say 'I've Just…'

The expression **venir de** is very useful. It expresses the idea of having just done something. For example:

- **Elle vient de voir ce film.**
  She's just seen this film.
- **Je viens de manger du pop-corn.**
  I've just eaten some popcorn.

In the imperfect **venir de** means 'had just'.

- **Je venais de finir.** I had just finished.

✓ Maximise Your Marks

When talking about your pastimes, try and extend the length of your sentences to include as much extra detail as you can. **Je joue au foot** is correct French, but you can easily make the phrase more interesting by putting in such details as when, where, who with and so on. **Je joue au foot deux fois par semaine avec mes copains dans le parc** is a far more complex sentence and will gain extra marks.

❓ Test Yourself

What do these mean in English?
1. **Je suis sortie avec mes copines.**
2. **Elles adorent les comédies musicales.**

How do you say these in French?
3. I saw the film last Saturday.
4. They went to the concert last night.

⭐ Stretch Yourself

1. Say or write in French: 'My friend had just gone out when I phoned him.'
2. Say or write in French: 'I don't like films. They are becoming boring.'

More Leisure Activities

Watching TV

une émission	programme
le petit écran	small screen
les informations	news
les actualités	news
la météo	weather forecast
un documentaire	documentary
une émission pour les enfants	children's programme
une émission sportive	sports programme
une émission musicale	music programme
un feuilleton	soap
une série	series
une série policière	detective programme
la publicité	adverts
un jeu	game show
une chaîne	TV channel
la télé par satellite	satellite TV
la télé par câble	cable TV
haute définition	HD (high definition)
un écran plat	flat screen
numérique	digital
enregistreur à disque dur	digital recorder
un lecteur DVD	DVD player

Je n'aime pas regarder la télé. Il y a trop de feuilletons et de télé-réalité.
I don't like watching TV. There are too many soaps and reality TV programmes.

Je regarde la télé tous les jours. J'aime surtout les informations et les documentaires sur les animaux.
I watch TV every day. I particularly like the news and documentaries on animals.

Je trouve qu'il y a trop de publicité à la télé.
I think there is too much advertising on TV.

Reading and Music

J'adore la lecture. Je passe beaucoup de temps à lire des livres.
I love reading. I spend a lot of time reading books.

J'apprécie surtout les romans historiques et les bandes dessinées.
I especially appreciate historical novels and cartoons.

Je lis des magazines parce que je m'intéresse aux articles sur la mode et le courrier du cœur.
I read magazines because I'm interested in the articles on fashion and the problem page.

Note that **jouer** à is used for games and sports. For example:
- **Je joue au Scrabble.** I play Scrabble.

But, for musical instruments, you have to use **jouer de**. For example:
- **Je joue du piano depuis deux ans.** I've been playing the piano for two years.
- **Mon ami aime jouer de la flûte.** My friend likes playing the flute.

Here are some useful words for talking about which musical instruments you play.

le violon	violin	**la batterie**	drums
la guitare	guitar	**le clavier**	keyboard
la trompette	trumpet	**la clarinette**	clarinet
la flûte	flute	**le saxophone**	saxophone
le piano	piano	**le hautbois**	oboe

J'aime la musique de toutes sortes mais surtout le jazz.
I like all kinds of music, but especially jazz.

Je ne peux pas supporter le rap – je le trouve monotone.
I can't stand rap music – I find it monotonous.

Mon chanteur favori est...parce qu'il a une belle voix et j'aime les paroles de ses chansons.
My favourite singer is...because he has a lovely voice and I like the words/lyrics of his songs.

Build Your Skills: Possessive Pronouns

The possessive pronouns are 'mine', 'yours', 'his', 'hers', 'ours' and 'theirs'.

mine	le mien, la mienne, les miens, les miennes
yours (singular)	le tien, la tienne, les tiens, les tiennes
his / hers	le sien, la sienne, les siens, les siennes
ours	le nôtre, la nôtre, les nôtres
yours (plural or polite)	le vôtre, la vôtre, les vôtres
theirs	le leur, la leur, les leurs

In French, these words have a masculine singular form, a feminine singular form, a masculine plural form and a feminine plural form. Note that the French for 'ours', 'yours' and 'theirs' have only one plural form (for masculine and feminine).

C'est à qui, ce livre? Whose book is this?
C'est le mien. It's mine.
C'est à qui, cette guitare? Whose guitar is this?
C'est la mienne. It's mine.

In informal conversation, you can often convey the same idea by using the pronouns **moi**, **toi**, **lui**, **elle**, **nous**, **vous**, **eux** and **elles**. For example:
- **C'est à moi.** It's mine.

Asking People Out

Here are some useful phrases for asking people to go out with you.

Tu veux aller au cinéma avec moi?
Do you want to go to the cinema with me?

Tu as envie de jouer au badminton?
Do you feel like playing badminton?

Tu peux venir au concert?
Can you come to the concert?

If you want to refuse:
Je ne peux pas	I can't
Je ne veux pas	I don't want to
Non, merci	No thanks!
Fiche-moi la paix!	Get lost!

Je dois me laver les cheveux.
I must wash my hair.

If you want to accept:
Oui, je veux bien	Yes, I'd like that
Avec plaisir	With pleasure
Pourquoi pas?	Why not?

On se retrouve où? Et à quelle heure?
Where shall we meet? And what time?

On se retrouve devant le cinéma à sept heures, d'accord?
We'll meet in front of the cinema at 7, OK?

✓ Maximise Your Marks

To gain an A or an A*, you need to give reasons for anything you say or write. For example:
- **Je vais souvent à des concerts parce que j'aime sortir avec mes amis.**
  I often go to concerts because I like going out with my friends.

❓ Test Yourself

What do these mean in English?
1. **Tu as envie de manger chez moi?**
2. **Elle vient de commencer à apprendre à jouer de la batterie.**

How do you say these in French?
3. Do you want to go for a walk?
4. No thanks. I have to wash my hair.

★ Stretch Yourself

1. Say or write in French: 'I found a pen. She says it's hers but I think that it's yours.'

2. Say or write in French: 'Whose is that flute? It's mine.'

Shopping

At the Shops

une bijouterie	jeweller's	Le prix est bon?	Is it a good price?
une boucherie	butcher's	C'est combien?	How much is it?
une boulangerie	baker's		
une charcuterie	delicatessen	Ça fait combien?	How much does it come to?
une confiserie	sweet shop		
une épicerie	grocer's	une offre spéciale	a special offer
un grand magasin	department store	une réduction	a reduction
un hypermarché	hypermarket	des rabais	reductions
une laiterie	dairy	cher/pas cher	expensive/cheap
un marchand de légumes	greengrocer's	bon marché	cheap
le marché	market	élevé/bas	high/low
une parfumerie	perfume shop	en hausse/en baisse	up/down
une pâtisserie	cake shop	une augmentation	an increase
une poissonnerie	fishmonger's	la monnaie	change
une quincaillerie	hardware shop	un billet (de banque)	bank note
le rayon alimentation	food department	une pièce de monnaie	coin
un supermarché	supermarket	des livres sterling	(British) pounds sterling
un magasin de vêtements	clothes shop	un portefeuille	wallet
		un porte-monnaie	purse

Je peux vous aider? Vous désirez?
Can I help you? What would you like?

Je cherche le rayon des vêtements hommes.
I'm looking for the men's department.

C'est au troisième étage/au sous-sol/au rez-de-chaussée.
It's on the third floor/in the basement/on the ground floor.

L'escalier roulant ne marche pas. Où est l'ascenseur?
The escalator isn't working. Where is the lift?

Où est la caisse? Où sont les soldes?
Where is the till? Where are the sales?

Je veux me plaindre. Je voudrais un remboursement.
I want to complain. I'd like a refund.

✓ Maximise Your Marks

Here are a few more very useful connectives: **car** (since/because), **donc** (so), **d'une part** (on the one hand), **d'autre part** (on the other hand), **en revanche** (on the other hand) and **d'ailleurs** (moreover).

More on Adjectives

Most adjectives form their feminine by adding
–e but there are also many irregular adjectives:

Adjectives ending in –f change to –ve in the
feminine form. For example:
- **un magasin neuf** a new shop
- **une épicerie neuve** a new grocer's

Adjectives ending in –x change to –se in the
feminine form. For example:
- **Il est heureux.** He is happy.
- **Elle est heureuse.** She is happy.

Adjectives ending in –n often double the n and
add –e in the feminine form. For example:
- **Le restaurant est moyen.**
  The restaurant is average.
- **Elle est de taille moyenne.**
  She is of average height.

Note these other irregular adjectives:

frais/fraîche (cool, fresh):
- **le fromage frais**   fresh cheese
- **de l'eau fraîche**   fresh water

sec/sèche (dry):
- **un vin sec**   a dry wine
- **une pomme sèche**   a dry apple

blanc/blanche (white):
- **un vin blanc**   a white wine
- **la viande blanche**   white meat

long/longue (long):
- **un long voyage**   a long journey
- **une longue visite**   a long visit

💡 Boost Your Memory

Take care when learning vocabulary with
so-called **faux amis** (false friends), that is
words which look like English words but
have a different meaning. For example, **une
veste** does *not* mean vest, it is a 'jacket';
un magasin is a 'shop' *not* a magazine.
Words like **travailler** (to work) and **la
journée** (the day) also cause problems.

Make a list and add new false friends to it
as you find them, for example **un car**
= a coach.

Build Your Skills: This and That

To say 'this'/'that' and 'these'/'those' in
French, you use **ce**, **cette** and **ces**.

In front of a masculine word, use **ce**:
- **Ce magasin est ouvert.** This shop is open.

In front of a feminine word, use **cette**:
- **Cette pomme est délicieuse.**
  This apple is delicious.

In front of a plural word, use **ces**, whether the
word is masculine or feminine:
- **Ces magasins sont fermés.**
  These shops are closed.
- **Ces pommes sont vieilles.**
  Those apples are old.

For masculine words beginning with a vowel or
silent **h**, there is a special form of **ce**:
- **Cet œuf est dur.** This egg is hard.
- **Cet homme cherche de l'eau minérale.**
  That man is looking for mineral water.

If you need to distinguish between 'this' and
'that', you can add –**ci** (this) or –**là** (that) to the
end of the word. For example:
- **Ce magasin-ci est ouvert, mais ce magasin-là
  est fermé.**
  This shop is open but that shop is closed.
- **Ces poissons-ci sont frais mais ces poissons-
  là sentent mauvais.**
  These fish are fresh but those fish smell off.

❓ Test Yourself

What do these mean in English?
1. **Cet ascenseur ne marche pas.**
2. **Ce supermarché est moderne mais très cher.**

How do you say these in French?
3. This new shop is closed on Sundays.
4. I'm looking for a special offer.

⭐ Stretch Yourself

1. Say or write in French: 'This purse is
   pretty but that wallet is less expensive.'

2. Say or write in French: 'These shops are
   good but those shops are cheaper.'

Fashion

Buying Clothes

un blouson	jacket
une casquette	cap
un chapeau	hat
des chaussettes	socks
des chaussures	shoes
une chemise	shirt
un costume	suit
une cravate	tie
un imperméable	raincoat
une jupe	skirt
un jogging	tracksuit
un maillot de bain	bathing suit
un manteau	coat
une montre	watch
un pantalon	trousers
un pull	jumper
une robe	dress
un sac à main	handbag
un short	shorts
un tee-shirt	T-shirt
une veste	jacket

en coton	(made of) cotton
en cuir	(made of) leather
en soie	(made of) silk
en laine	(made of) wool
en jean	(made of) denim
en velours	(made of) velvet/corduroy
écossais	tartan

étroit	tight
uni	plain
à rayures	with stripes/stripy
à pois	with spots, spotted
à carreaux	checked
large	baggy
court	short
long	long

Je cherche une chemise en coton.
I'm looking for a cotton shirt.

Vous faites quelle taille?
What size are you?

Je cherche des baskets.
I'm looking for trainers.

Vous faites quelle pointure?
What shoe size are you?

Je peux l'essayer/les essayer?
Can I try it/them on?

Où est la cabine d'essayage?
Where is the changing room?

Avez-vous la même chemise en bleu?
Have you got the same shirt in blue?

Je regrette, il n'y en a plus.
I'm sorry, we haven't got any more/don't have any left.

What Is Your Look?

Elle aime le look gothique. Elle porte des vêtements sombres et des bottes noires.
She likes the goth look. She wears dark clothes and black boots.

Il aime mieux le look rappeur. Il porte un tee-shirt large et un pantalon trop long avec des baskets blanches.
He prefers the rapper look. He wears a baggy T-shirt and trousers that are too long with white trainers.

Pour aller en vacances elle va acheter un bikini, des jupes et des lunettes de soleil.
To go on holiday, she's going to buy a bikini, some skirts and some sunglasses.

Pour assister au mariage de sa sœur, elle va mettre une robe blanche et des chaussures noires.
To attend her sister's wedding, she's going to wear a white dress and black shoes.

Lifestyle

Build Your Skills: Asking and Answering 'Which One(s)?'

To ask 'which one?' or to say 'this one', etc, you need to know the gender of the word you are talking about.

To ask 'which one?', you need to use **lequel/laquelle/lesquels/lesquelles**:

Masculine singular:
Il y a beaucoup de pulls. Lequel préfères-tu?
There are lots of jumpers. Which one do you prefer?

Feminine singular:
Il y a un grand choix de robes. Laquelle préfères-tu?
There's a big choice of dresses. Which one do you prefer?

Masculine plural:
Je n'aime pas ces tee-shirts. Lesquels?
I don't like those T-shirts. Which ones?

Feminine plural:
J'ai choisi des chaussettes. Lesquelles?
I've chosen some socks. Which ones?

To say 'this one', 'that one', 'these ones' or 'those ones', you need to use the following:

Masculine singular:	Feminine singular:
ce **pull** this jumper	cette **veste** this jacket
celui-ci this one	celle-ci this one
celui-là that one	celle-là that one
Masculine plural:	Feminine plural:
ces **chapeaux** these hats	ces **chaussures** these shoes
ceux-ci these (ones)	
ceux-là those (ones)	celles-ci these (ones)
	celles-là those (ones)

The Verb 'Mettre'

The verb **mettre** (to put/to put on) is irregular. Here is the present tense in full:

Je mets	I put, am putting (on)
Tu mets	You put, are putting (on)
Il/Elle met	He/She puts, is putting (on)
Nous mettons	We put, are putting (on)
Vous mettez	You put, are putting (on)
Ils/Elles mettent	They put, are putting (on)

Je mets mon nouveau blouson.
I'm putting on my new jacket.

Elle met un pantalon parce qu'elle n'aime pas porter des jupes.
She's putting on trousers because she doesn't like wearing skirts.

The past participle of the verb **mettre** is **mis**. For example:

Ils ont mis leurs meilleurs vêtements.
They've put on their best clothes.

✓ Maximise Your Marks

Take care with the meaning of some reflexive verbs.
- **mettre** means 'to put' or 'put on': **je mets mon chapeau** (I'm putting on my hat)
- **se mettre à** means 'to start': **je me mets à économiser** (I'm starting to save)
- **plaindre** means 'to pity' or 'feel sorry (for)'
- **se plaindre** means 'to complain'

❓ Test Yourself

What do these mean in English?
1. **Cette chemise est trop grande.**
2. **Ce pantalon n'est pas trop cher.**

How do you say these in French?
3. I'm looking for a long cotton T-shirt.
4. I'm wearing black, leather shoes.

⭐ Stretch Yourself

1. Say or write in French: 'Here are some dresses. Which ones do you prefer? These or those?'

2. Say or write in French: 'Which jumper do you prefer? This one or that one?'

New Technology and the Media

Lifestyle

Computers and the Internet

un ordinateur	computer
un ordinateur portable	laptop
le logiciel	software
une imprimante	printer
un clavier	keyboard
une souris	mouse
une cartouche	ink cartridge
un disque compact	CD
une clé USB	USB memory stick
un courriel	email message
l'e-mail	email
une adresse	address
un lien	link
un forum	newsgroup
la toile	the web
un site	site
cliquer	to click
le serveur	server
tchatcher/chatter	to chat
un blog	blog

Je passe beaucoup de temps sur mon ordinateur. J'envoie des e-mail, je télécharge des vidéoclips et je joue aux jeux.
I spend a lot of time on my computer. I send emails, download videos and play games.

Je surfe sur Internet pour trouver des renseignements pour m'aider avec mes devoirs.
I surf the Internet to find information to help me with my homework.

Pour moi, le réseau social est indispensable.
For me, social networking is indispensable.

On peut acheter des choses à des prix très bas, mais la fraude est un gros problème.
You can buy things at low prices, but fraud is a big problem.

Les enfants peuvent rencontrer des gens malhonnêtes s'ils ne sont pas surveillés.
Children can meet dishonest people if they are not supervised.

Advertising

un spot publicitaire	a TV advert
les petites annonces	classified ads
une page de publicité	radio advert/ commercial break
vanter	to boast
encourager	to encourage
exagérer	to exaggerate
mentir	to lie
une vedette	a star/celebrity
destiné à	aimed at
le/la meilleur(e)	the best
un slogan	slogan
la cible	the target (audience)

La publicité encourage les gens à acheter les choses dont ils n'ont pas besoin.
Advertising encourages people to buy things that they don't need.

La publicité est utile parce qu'elle donne des renseignements aux consommateurs.
Advertising is useful because it gives consumers information.

MP3 Players

Mon lecteur MP3 n'a pas beaucoup de mémoire et je dois recharger les piles tous les jours.
My MP3 player hasn't got much memory and I have to recharge the batteries every day.

Ma sœur a un lecteur MP3 qui est très léger avec un écran tactile. Elle peut facilement télécharger des vidéoclips gratuitement.
My sister has an MP3 player that is very light and has a touch screen. She can download videos easily for free.

Mobile Phones

mon téléphone portable	my mobile phone
un texto	text
téléphone prépayé	pay-as-you-go phone
téléphone avec forfait	contract
un appareil	camera
une carte mémoire	SIM card
Internet haut débit	broadband
une facture	a bill
une sonnerie	ring tone
gratuit	free
le GPS	sat-nav
équipé de…	equipped with…

Je ne peux pas vivre sans mon portable.
I can't live without my mobile.

La facture est très chère.
The bill is very expensive.

Les portables sont utiles pour la sécurité mais dans un train les gens qui parlent au téléphone sont vraiment énervants.
Mobiles are useful for safety, but people who talk on the phone on trains are really annoying.

Les portables sont dangereux pour le cerveau.
Mobile phones are dangerous for the brain.

Certaines sonneries sont nulles.
Some ring tones are awful.

Build Your Skills: Relative Pronouns

You have already met the relative pronouns **qui** and **que**. For example:

- **J'ai un nouveau portable** qui **a un appareil cinq megapixels.** I have a new phone, which has a 5-megapixel camera.
- **C'est le portable** que **ses parents lui ont offert.** That's the phone that his parents gave him.

In the previous sentences, **qui** and **que** both replace the word 'phone'. But, when you want to replace a whole sentence or clause, you need to use **ce qui** or **ce que** instead. For example:

- **J'ai un portable prépayé,** ce qui **est plus pratique pour moi.** I have a pay-as-you-go phone, which is more practical for me.
- **Les appels de l'étranger sont très chers,** ce que **je trouve inacceptable.** Calls from abroad are very expensive, which I find unacceptable.

? Test Yourself

What do these mean in English?
1. **Il y a trop de publicité à la télé.**
2. **Les textos sont gratuits pour moi.**

How do you say these in French?
3. I play games on my computer.
4. My new computer is much faster.

★ Stretch Yourself

1. Say or write in French: 'Mobiles are dangerous, which is worrying.'

2. Say or write in French: 'He spends a lot of time on the computer, which is boring.'

Lifestyle

Events and Celebrations

Events to Celebrate

le Nouvel An	New Year
la Saint-Sylvestre	New Year's Eve
Noël	Christmas
la veille de Noël	Christmas Eve
l'arbre de Noël	Christmas tree
le père Noël	Father Christmas
Pâques	Easter
la fête nationale	Bastille Day
le quatorze juillet	the 14th of July
Dipavali	Diwali
Aïd	Eid
Hannoukah	Hanukkah
le Nouvel An chinois	Chinese New Year
l'anniversaire	birthday
une fête	party
un jour férié	bank holiday
le mariage	wedding
la naissance	the birth
la mort	the death
le baptême	Christening
les fiançailles	engagement
les noces (d'argent)	(silver) anniversary
C'est quand?	When is it?
au printemps	in spring
en été	in summer
en automne	in autumn
en hiver	in winter
en mars/octobre	in March/October
les feux d'artifice	firework display

un bal	a dance
un défilé	a procession
une carte	card
un cadeau	present
des bougies	candles
des lumières	lights
des chansons	songs

À Noël, on achète des cadeaux, on envoie des cartes, on décore la maison et on mange trop.
At Christmas, we buy gifts, send cards, decorate the house and eat too much.

Je reçois des cartes et des cadeaux.
I receive cards and presents.

Le quatorze juillet, il y a un défilé et le soir il y a un bal dans la rue avec des feux d'artifice.
On the 14th of July, there's a procession and in the evening a street party and firework display.

À Dipavali, on offre des cadeaux, on illumine la maison et on mange des choses sucrées.
At Diwali, we give presents, light up the house and eat sweet things.

À Hannoukah, on allume chaque soir une bougie et on joue à des jeux. On mange des crêpes et des beignets.
At Hanukkah, we light a candle each evening and play games. We eat pancakes and doughnuts.

Build Your Skills: Reflexive Verbs in the Perfect Tense

All reflexive verbs (e.g. **se lever**, **se coucher**) take **être** in the perfect tense. Here is the perfect tense of the reflexive verb **s'amuser** (to have a good time) in full:

Je me suis amusé(e)	I had a good time
Tu t'es amusé(e)	You had a good time
Il s'est amusé	He had a good time
Elle s'est amusée	She had a good time
Nous nous sommes amusé(e)s	We had a good time
Vous êtes amusé(e)(s)(es)	You had a good time
Ils se sont amusés	They had a good time
Elles se sont amusées	They had a good time

Lifestyle

Au Nouvel An, on a fait le réveillon et je me suis couchée **très tard.**
At New Year, we had a party and I went to bed very late.

À la fin du Ramadan, je me suis habillé **de mes nouveaux vêtements pour fêter l'Aïd.**
At the end of Ramadan, I got dressed in my new clothes to celebrate Eid.

Au Nouvel An chinois, on a nettoyé la maison et on a mis de nouveaux vêtements. On a mangé un grand repas en famille. Nous nous sommes amusés.
At Chinese New Year, we cleaned the house and put on new clothes. We ate a large family meal. We had a good time.

The Superlative

As you have seen already (page 13), to make comparisons you use **plus** or **moins** with an adjective + **que**. For example:

- **La fête nationale est plus amusante que le Nouvel An.**
  Bastille Day is more enjoyable than New Year.
- **Les cartes sont moins intéressantes que les cadeaux.**
  Cards are less interesting than presents.

Plus means 'more' and **moins** means 'less'. If you want to say 'the most' or 'the least' you simply put **le** (masculine singular), **la** (feminine singular) or **les** (plural) in front of **plus** or **moins**. For example:

- **Mon portable est le plus chic.**
  My phone is the smartest (most smart).
- **Ce village est le moins connu de France.**
  It is the least well-known village in France.

Le meilleur/la meilleure/les meilleurs/les meilleures are used to say 'the best'. For example:
- **Les meilleurs feux d'artifice du monde.**
  The best fireworks in the world.

The French for 'the worst' is **le pire/la pire** or **les pires**. For example:
- **C'est la pire carte dans le magasin.**
  It is the worst card in the shop.

? Test Yourself

What do these mean in English?
1. Il a allumé les bougies.
2. Elle a reçu beaucoup de cadeaux.

How do you say these in French?
3. I ate too many chocolates at Easter.
4. I love eating pancakes.

★ Stretch Yourself

1. Say or write in French: 'I didn't have a good time because I argued with my girlfriend.'

2. Say or write in French: 'The boys went to bed late but they had a good time.'

Sport and Exercise

Sports

l'alpinisme	mountaineering
l'athlétisme	athletics
le basket	basketball
courir	to run
la course	running
le cyclisme	cycling
la danse	dance
l'escalade	climbing
l'équitation	horse-riding
le foot	football
le golf	golf
la gymnastique	gymnastics
le handball	handball
la musculation	bodybuilding
la natation	swimming
le patin à roulettes	roller-skating
patiner	to skate
la pêche	fishing
le ping-pong	table tennis
la planche à voile	windsurfing
les promenades	walks
les randonnées	walks/hikes
le skate	skateboarding
le ski nautique	waterskiing
les sports d'hiver	winter sports
le tennis	tennis

Il aime jouer au foot. Il marque beaucoup de buts.
He likes playing football. He scores a lot of goals.

Elle fait souvent de la gymnastique. Elle a adhéré à un club.
She often does gymnastics. She has joined a club.

Je vais à la pêche avec mon père.
I go fishing with my father.

Je fais de la natation parce que c'est bon pour la santé.
I swim because it's good for your health.

Il est important de participer aux sports. Le sport est relaxant et on se sent mieux.
It is important to take part in sports. Sport is relaxing and you feel better.

C'est bon pour le cœur et cela aide à perdre du poids.
It's good for the heart and it helps you to lose weight.

C'est sociable. On se fait de nouveaux amis surtout si on joue en équipe.
It's sociable. You make new friends especially if you play in a team.

Je n'aime pas perdre. Je trouve la défaite difficile.
I don't like to lose. I find defeat hard to take.

J'aime gagner. La victoire est satisfaisante.
I like winning. Victory is satisfying.

J'ai vu un match nul samedi. C'était ennuyeux.
I saw a draw on Saturday. It was boring.

Build Your Skills: Saying When You Are Doing Something

You can use the expressions **venir de**, **être en train de** and **être sur le point de** to be specific about when you have done, are doing or will do an activity.

You use **venir de** in the present tense to convey that you have just done something. For example:
- **Je** viens de **jouer au rugby.**
  I've just played rugby.
- **Tu** viens de **finir?** Have you just finished?

- **Il/Elle** vient de **faire de la voile.**
  He/She has just been sailing.
- **Nous** venons de **gagner le jeu.**
  We've just won the game.
- **Vous** venez de **me battre.**
  You've just beaten me.
- **Ils/Elles** viennent de **perdre le match.**
  They've just lost the match.

Build Your Skills (cont.)

You use **être sur le point de** for something you are about to do. For example:

- **Je** suis sur le point de **partir pour le stade.**
  I'm about to set off for the stadium.

- **Ils** sont sur le point de **marquer un but.**
  They're about to score a goal.

You use **être en train de** for when you are in the middle of doing something. For example:

- **Il** est en train de **faire du vélo.**
  He's just out cycling.

- **Ils ne peuvent pas vous voir. Ils** sont en train de **manger.**
  They can't see you. They're in the middle of eating.

The Present Participle

To form the present participle, take the **nous** form of the present tense, remove the **–ons** and add **–ant**.

When it is used after the preposition **en**, the present participle means 'in', 'on', 'by' or 'while'. For example:

Je garde la forme en faisant du sport.
I keep fit by doing sport.

Je fais du jogging en écoutant de la musique.
I jog while listening to music.

En arrivant au gymnase, il a fait des exercices.
On arriving at the gym, he did some exercises.

Je suis tombé en jouant au basket.
I fell while playing basketball.

💡 Boost Your Memory

A common mistake is in mistranslating the English 'for' in time expressions.

Only use **pour** for something that has not happened yet:

- **Je vais partir en vacances pour huit jours.**
  I'm going to go on holiday for a week.

If you no longer do something, use **pendant**:

- **J'ai joué au squash pendant deux ans.**
  I played squash for two years.

If you still do the activity, use **depuis**:

- **Je fais du cyclisme depuis dix ans.**
  I've been cycling for 10 years.

So, when revising time expressions, ask yourself: is it all over? (if yes – **pendant**), is it still happening? (if yes – **depuis**), or is it yet to happen? (if yes – **pour**).

❓ Test Yourself

What do these mean in English?
1. **Je ne joue pas au rugby. C'est violent.**
2. **Ils ont perdu le match.**

How do you say these in French?
3. I listen to music while jogging.
4. He loves playing tennis in the park.

⭐ Stretch Yourself

1. Say or write in French: 'I was just about to phone you when you arrived.'

2. Say or write in French: 'He's in the middle of doing his homework.'

A Healthy Lifestyle

Pains and Illnesses

Qu'est-ce qui ne va pas?
What's wrong?

Here are some useful phrases to use if you are not feeling well:

Je suis malade	I'm ill
Je ne me sens pas bien	I don't feel well
J'ai la grippe	I've got flu
Je suis enrhumé(e)	I've got a cold
J'ai de la fièvre	I have a temperature
Je tousse	I'm coughing
J'éternue	I'm sneezing
J'ai mal au cœur	I feel sick
Je ne dors pas	I'm not sleeping

Je ne mange pas	I'm not eating
J'ai perdu l'appétit	I've lost my appetite
Ça fait mal	It hurts
La jambe me fait mal	My leg hurts

J'ai...	I have...
mal au dos	backache
mal au cou/bras	a sore neck/arm
mal au pied/genou	a sore foot/knee
mal au doigt/nez	a sore finger/nose
mal au ventre	stomach ache
mal à l'estomac	stomach ache
mal à la tête	a headache
mal à la gorge/bouche	a sore throat/mouth
mal à l'épaule	a sore shoulder
mal à l'oreille	earache
mal à l'œil	a sore eye
mal aux yeux	sore eyes
mal aux dents	toothache
mal aux oreilles	earache

Fit and Active or Couch Potato?

Je me lève tôt et je fais de l'exercice.
I get up early and do some exercise.

Je promène le chien et je vais au travail à pied.
I walk the dog and I go to work on foot.

Je vais au gymnase tous les soirs.
I go to the gym every evening.

Je ne regarde pas la télé et je me couche toujours de bonne heure.
I don't watch TV and I always go to bed early.

Je fais la grasse matinée et je ne fais pas d'exercice.
I have a lie-in and don't do any exercise.

Je vais au travail en voiture.
I go to work by car.

Je ne vais pas au gymnase.
I don't go to the gym.

Je fume vingt cigarettes par jour.
I smoke 20 cigarettes a day.

Je regarde la télé tous les soirs et je me couche très tard.
I watch TV every night and go to bed very late.

Lifestyle

Build Your Skills: Negative Expressions

The basic way to make a verb negative is to put **ne...pas** around the verb. For example:

Je ne **sais** pas.　　　I don't know.

But here are some more negative expressions:

ne...**rien**	nothing
ne...**jamais**	never
ne...**plus**	no/any longer
ne...**personne**	nobody/no one
Je ne **fume** jamais.	I never smoke.

Some more useful negatives are **nulle part** (nowhere), **ne...que** (only), **aucun/aucune** (none/no). For example:

* **Il n'est pas sportif. Il** ne **va** jamais nulle part. **Il aime mieux rester chez lui.**
  He's not sporty. He never goes anywhere. He prefers staying at home.
* Aucun **joueur** n'**a marqué de but. C'était un match nul ennuyeux.**
  No player scored a goal. It was a boring draw.
* **Il** ne **fume** que **deux cigarettes par jour.** He only smokes two cigarettes a day.

Some negatives can be used as the subject of a verb. For example:

* Personne n'**a gagné.**
  No one won.
* Rien n'**a changé**.
  Nothing's changed.

In the perfect tense, you have to make **avoir** negative (i.e. the negative expression 'wraps around' **avoir**). For example:

* **Je** n'**ai** jamais **fumé.**
  I have never smoked.
* **Ils** n'**ont** rien **vu.**
  They saw nothing./They didn't see anything.

But note the exception **ne...personne**. When you use **ne...personne** or **ne...que**, the main verb (e.g. **vu**) splits the expression. For example:

* **Je** n'**ai vu** personne.
  I didn't see anyone.

Note how **un**, **une**, **du**, **de la** and **des** change to **de** (or **d'**) after a negative expression. For example:

* **Je fume** des **cigarettes.**
  I smoke cigarettes.
* **Je** ne **fume** pas de **cigarettes.**
  I don't smoke cigarettes.

? Test Yourself

What do these mean in English?
1. **Je ne joue pas au rugby. Ce n'est pas amusant.**
2. **Il a mal aux dents et il a de la fièvre.**

How do you say these in French?
3. I go to bed early and do a lot of exercise.
4. He eats too much. He is always hungry.

⭐ Stretch Yourself

1. Say or write in French: 'My friend never listens to me any more and no one can persuade her to change.'

2. Say or write in French: 'He only drinks once a week.'

Smoking, Drugs and Alcohol

Lifestyle

Smoking

Je fume des cigarettes.
I smoke cigarettes.

Je ne fume pas.
I don't smoke.

Je fume depuis deux ans.
I've been smoking for two years.

Je le trouve relaxant.
I find it relaxing.

C'est sociable.
It's sociable.

Cela combat le stress.
It fights stress.

Cela aide à mincir.
It helps you lose weight.

Cela cause le cancer du poumon.
It causes lung cancer.

Le tabagisme passif est dangereux pour les non-fumeurs.
Passive smoking is dangerous for non-smokers.

Ça pue et les vêtements sentent mauvais.
It stinks and your clothes smell bad.

On a les dents et les doigts jaunes.
You get yellow teeth and fingers.

Alcohol

Je ne bois jamais; c'est dangereux pour le foie.
I never drink; it's dangerous for the liver.

Mon père boit de la bière avec modération.
My father drinks beer in moderation.

Il y a des jeunes qui boivent excessivement.
There are some young people who drink excessively.

On boit pour être sociable.
People drink to be sociable.

L'alcool provoque des accidents de la route.
Alcohol causes road accidents.

Drugs

un(e) drogué(e)	a drug addict
la désintoxication	rehabilitation
un comprimé	tablet
une piqûre	injection
piquer	to inject
une drogue douce	soft drug
une drogue dure	hard drug
une drogue illicite	illegal drug
le cannabis	cannabis
la cocaïne	cocaine
l'ecstasy	ecstasy
l'héroïne	heroin

La drogue est un gros problème. Il est facile de devenir accro.
Drugs are a big problem. It's easy to become addicted.

La drogue cause la criminalité. Il y a un lien entre la drogue et la criminalité.
Drugs lead to crime. Drugs and crime are linked.

Les jeunes sont tentés par la drogue parce que c'est interdit.
Young people are tempted by drugs because they're illegal.

Ils croient qu'il est cool de consommer de la drogue. Ils prennent de la drogue pour faire comme les autres.
They think it's cool to take drugs. They take drugs to be like others.

Ils se droguent à cause de la pression des pairs.
They take drugs because of peer pressure.

On ne connaît pas toutes les conséquences à long terme de la toxicomanie.
We don't know what the long-term consequences of addiction are.

Les toxicomanes ne peuvent pas se passer de drogue.
Addicts cannot do without drugs.

Build Your Skills: The Subjunctive

After certain expressions, such as **bien que** (although), **pour que** (so that), **pourvu que** (provided that), **à moins que** (unless) and **il faut que** (it is necessary that), you have to use a special form of the verb known as the subjunctive. You have no need to use it for GCSE, but you may come across it in reading and listening texts.

Here is the verb **être** in the subjunctive:

Que je sois	I am
Que tu sois	You are
Qu'il/Qu'elle soit	He/She is
Que nous soyons	We are
Que vous soyez	You are
Qu'ils/Qu'elles soient	They are

Je fume bien que ce soit dangereux.
I smoke, although it is dangerous.

–er verbs are the same in the subjunctive except for the **nous** and **vous** forms, which are the same as the imperfect:

Il faut qu'il arrête de fumer.
He must stop smoking.

Il faut que vous évitiez la drogue.
You must avoid drugs.

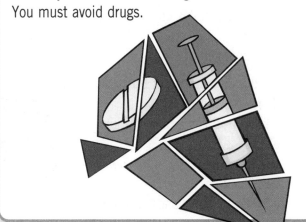

Other common irregular subjunctive verbs are:
Que je fasse (faire)
Que j'aie (avoir)
Que j'aille (aller)
Que je puisse (pouvoir)

Je ne bois jamais d'alcool pour que je puisse rester en bonne forme.
I never drink alcohol so that I can stay healthy.

✓ Maximise Your Marks

Always remember to check the endings of adjectives to make sure you have made them agree.

L'alcool est dangereux (alcohol is dangerous) but **la drogue est dangereuse.**

Les cigarettes sont mauvaises pour la santé (cigarettes are bad for you) but **les fruits sont bons pour la santé.**

❓ Test Yourself

What do these mean in English?
1. **Il fume environ dix cigarettes par jour.**
2. **Elle boit trop souvent; c'est mauvais pour le foie.**

How do you say these in French?
3. Young people think it is cool to smoke.
4. Heroin is a dangerous drug.

⭐ Stretch Yourself

1. Fill in the gaps with the correct form of the verb:

   Il faut que j'.... chez lui (use **aller**) **pour que je ......** (use **pouvoir**) **mettre mon manteau bien qu'il ne... pas** (use **faire**) **froid.**

2. Say or write in French: 'He smokes, although it is dangerous.'

Food and Drink

Fruit and Vegetables

> **Il faut manger cinq portions de fruits et de légumes tous les jours.**
> You should eat five portions of fruit and veg every day.

un abricot	apricot
un ananas	pineapple
une banane	banana
une cerise	cherry
un citron	lemon
une fraise	strawberry
une framboise	raspberry
un kiwi	kiwi fruit
du melon	melon
une orange	orange
un pamplemousse	grapefruit
une pêche	peach
une poire	pear
une pomme	apple
une prune	plum
du raisin	grapes
une tomate	tomato
une carotte	carrot
un chou	cabbage
un chou-fleur	cauliflower
un concombre	cucumber
des haricots verts	green beans
des petits pois	peas
une pomme de terre	potato
un radis	radish
une salade	lettuce/salad

How to Say 'Some' and 'Any'

Masculine words take **du**:
- **Je voudrais du chou.** I'd like some cabbage.

Feminine words take **de la**:
- **Je veux de la salade.** I want some salad.

Plural words take **des**:
- **Je mange des poires.** I'm eating some pears.

Words beginning with a vowel take **de l'**, whether the word is masculine or feminine. For example:
- **Je prends de l'ananas.** I'm having some pineapple.

In questions, **du**, **de la**, **des** and **de l'** are often translated as 'any'. For example:
- **Avez-vous des haricots verts?** Have you any beans?

Note what happens when you are giving quantities of food:
- **du**, **de la** and **des** change to **de** (or **d'** before a vowel)
- **de l'** changes to **d'**

- **un kilo de pommes et 500 grammes de fromage**
  a kilo of apples and half a kilo of cheese
- **une bouteille d'eau et un morceau de gâteau**
  a bottle of water and a piece of cake

Healthy and Unhealthy Diets

Les jeunes boivent trop d'alcool.
Young people drink too much alcohol.

J'évite de manger trop de chocolat.
I avoid eating too much chocolate.

Nous essayons de manger équilibré.
We try to eat a balanced diet.

Il faut boire beaucoup d'eau.
You should drink lots of water.

C'est trop gras. Il ne faut pas consommer trop de graisse.
It's too fatty. One/You shouldn't consume too much fat.

Il faut éviter trop de produits laitiers.
You should avoid too many dairy products.

Il ne faut pas consommer trop de graisse, de sucre ou de sel.
You shouldn't have too much fat, sugar or salt.

At the Restaurant

Qu'est-ce que vous prenez?
What are you having?

L'addition, s'il vous plaît.
The bill, please.

les hors d'œuvre	starters
les entrées	starters
des crudités	raw vegetables
des fruits de mer	seafood
du saucisson	salami
du pâté	pâté
du jambon	ham
du potage	soup
de la soupe	soup
les plats principaux	main courses
du poulet	chicken
du poisson	fish
de la viande	meat
de l'agneau	lamb
du porc	pork
du steak	steak
une omelette	omelette
un œuf	egg
des frites	chips
les desserts	sweets/desserts
de la pâtisserie	pastry
des gâteaux	cakes
de la tarte	tart
du fromage	cheese
des glaces	ice cream
de la crème	cream
du café	coffee
du chocolat	chocolate
du thé	tea
de l'eau	water
du coca	cola
de la limonade	lemonade
du jus d'orange	orange juice
de la bière	beer
du vin	wine
du cidre	cider

Build Your Skills: The Pronoun 'En'

You will often find the word **en** used in a sentence to mean 'of it' or 'of them'. **En** always goes before the verb, for example:
- **Combien de tomates y a-t-il dans le frigo? Il y en a quatre.**
  How many tomatoes are there in the fridge? There are four (of them).
- **Le poisson est bon pour la santé. J'en mange une fois par semaine.**
  Fish is good for your health. I eat some (of it) once a week.

✓ Maximise Your Marks

Two very useful expressions are **on devrait** (one should, ought to) and **on pourrait** (one could, might). They are both followed by the infinitive.
- **On devrait éviter trop de sel.**
  One should avoid too much salt.

These are forms of the conditional tense. At GCSE, examiners would only expect candidates aiming for A or A* to use them.

? Test Yourself

What do these mean in English?
1. Il faut manger beaucoup de légumes.
2. Je n'aime pas la viande rouge. C'est trop gras.

How do you say these in French?
3. I try to eat a balanced diet.
4. She never eats red meat.

★ Stretch Yourself

1. Say or write in French: 'Milk is good for you. I drink some every day.'

2. Say or write in French: 'I like fruit. I eat some every morning.'

Lifestyle

Practice Questions

 Complete these exam-style questions to test your skills and understanding. Check your answers on page 93. You may wish to answer these questions on a separate piece of paper.

Reading

1 Read the passages below and answer the questions that follow.

Le week-end, j'aime aller à la piscine avec mes amies. J'adore nager, c'est bon pour la santé. Pascal	**Le week-end, j'aime faire de l'équitation. J'aime me promener à cheval à la campagne.** Élodie
Le week-end, je fais souvent du vélo avec mon ami, Robert. Pour mon anniversaire, je vais recevoir une nouvelle bicyclette. Richard	J'adore la lecture. Je préfère les livres de science-fiction, mais j'aime aussi lire des bandes dessinées et des romans d'aventures. Le samedi, je vais à la bibliothèque. Céline

  a) Who likes cycling?   .... (1)

  b) Who enjoys swimming?   .... (1)

  c) Who reads a lot?   .... (1)

  d) Who likes horse-riding?   .... (1)

  e) Who likes reading adventure novels?   .... (1)

  f) Who goes to the library?   .... (1)

2 Read what these people say about their eating habits and then answer the questions that follow.

Au petit déjeuner, je prends des céréales et généralement je bois du chocolat chaud. À midi, je rentre à la maison et je prends le déjeuner avec maman et ma petite sœur. Le soir, pour le dîner, je mange de la viande ou du poisson avec des légumes. Morgane	**Pour le petit déjeuner, je prends généralement du pain grillé avec de la confiture et un jus d'orange. Je prends le petit déjeuner dans la cuisine à sept heures. À l'heure du déjeuner, j'aime manger à la cantine au collège. Je préfère le steak-frites. Le soir, je ne mange pas beaucoup. On dîne vers huit heures.** Philippe
Je ne prends jamais de petit déjeuner. À midi je mange à la cantine scolaire. Je prends souvent une salade et un yaourt. Le soir, je dîne avec mes parents vers sept heures et demie. Je ne mange jamais de viande ni de poisson. Annie	

  a) What does Morgane have for breakfast?

  .... (2)

  b) What does she do for lunch?

  .... (1)

  c) What does Annie say about breakfast?

  .... (1)

d) Name one thing Annie eats regularly and one thing she does not eat.

....(2)

e) When and where does Philippe have his breakfast?

....(2)

f) What does he say about his evening meal?

....(1)

Speaking

3 You are talking about a recent shopping trip. Prepare to talk in French on the following points.

a) Say where you went.
b) Say why you went there.

....

c) Say what you bought.
d) Say what else you did.

....

e) Give your opinion of the day.
f) Say what you will do differently next time.

....(10)

Writing

4 Write an account about your lifestyle. Write about each of the following in French.

- What exercise you do
- What you have done recently to keep fit
- What you like to eat and drink, and why
- What you think about smoking and alcohol
- What you intend to do in the future to stay healthy

....

....

....

....

....(15)

Lifestyle

How well did you do?

| 1–13 | Try again | 14–23 | Getting there | 24–32 | Good work | 33–40 | Excellent! |

Travel

Countries

L'Allemagne	Germany
L'Angleterre	England
L'Australie	Australia
L'Autriche	Austria
La Belgique	Belgium
Le Canada	Canada
La Chine	China
Le Danemark	Denmark
L'Écosse	Scotland
L'Espagne	Spain
Les États-Unis	The United States/USA
La France	France
La Grande-Bretagne	Great Britain
La Grèce	Greece
L'Inde	India
L'Irlande	Ireland
L'Italie	Italy
Le Japon	Japan
Le Pakistan	Pakistan
Les Pays-Bas	The Netherlands/Holland
Le pays de Galles	Wales
Le Portugal	Portugal
La Russie	Russia
La Suisse	Switzerland

When you are talking about going to different countries, there are different ways to say 'to' or 'in', depending on whether the country is masculine, feminine or plural.

Masculine countries take **au**. For example:
- **Montréal se trouve au Canada.**
  Montreal is (situated) in Canada.

Feminine countries take **en**. For example:
- **Nous allons en Italie.**
  We're going to Italy.

Plural countries take **aux**. For example:
- **Je rêve d'aller aux États-Unis.**
  I dream of going to the United States.

Islands tend to take **à**. For example:
- **Je veux aller à Lanzarote.**
  I want to go to Lanzarote.

Nationalities

Allemand(e)	German
Anglais(e)	English
Australien(ne)	Australian
Autrichien(ne)	Austrian
Belge	Belgian
Canadien(ne)	Canadian
Chinois(e)	Chinese
Danois(e)	Danish
Écossais(e)	Scottish
Espagnol(e)	Spanish
Américain(e)	American
Français(e)	French
Britannique	British
Grec (Grecque)	Greek
Indien(ne)	Indian
Irlandais(e)	Irish
Italien(ne)	Italian
Japonais(e)	Japanese
Pakistanais(e)	Pakistani
Hollandais(e)	Dutch
Gallois(e)	Welsh
Portugais(e)	Portuguese
Russe	Russian
Suisse	Swiss

When talking about a person from a particular country, you use a capital letter – **un Italien, une Écossaise, les Français**. But you need to use a small letter when you are describing someone or something – **j'aime la cuisine italienne, il aime les montagnes écossaises, les garçons sont français**.

Holiday Destinations

à la campagne	to/at the country
au bord de la mer	to/at the seaside
à la montagne	to/at the mountains
en ville	to/in a city

J'aime aller en ville pour faire du lèche-vitrine et acheter des souvenirs.
I like going into town to go window-shopping and to buy souvenirs.

Holiday Destinations (cont.)

J'aime aller au bord de la mer parce que j'aime bronzer et me reposer. Je nage dans la mer et je fais de la voile et de la planche à voile.
I like going to the seaside because I like sunbathing and relaxing. I swim in the sea and I go sailing and windsurfing.

J'accompagne mes parents à la campagne et on loue une villa. J'adore le calme et j'oublie tout.
I go with my parents to the countryside and we hire/rent a villa. I love the calm and I forget everything.

Je vais à la montagne avec mes copains. On y va pour faire des sports d'hiver. I'm going to the mountains with my friends. We are going there to do winter sports.

Build Your Skills: The Pronoun 'Y'

The pronoun **y** means 'there'. It is very useful, but remember that it goes before the verb. For example:

- **J'adore l'Espagne. J'y vais tous les ans.**
  I love Spain. I go there every year.

- **Nous allons en Grèce cet été. Nous y allons en avion.**
  We're going to Greece this summer. We're going there by plane.

- **Ils partent aux États-Unis. Ils y vont en bateau.**
  They're going to the USA. They're going there by boat.

Prepositions

là-bas	over there
dedans	inside
dehors	outside
en bas	downstairs
en haut	upstairs
près de	near
loin de	a long way from/far from
contre	against
sauf	except
selon	according to
par	by/through
vers	towards/about (with time)
au bout de	at the end of
au fond de	at the back of
autour de	around

Où est la villa? C'est là-bas.
Where is the villa? It's over there.

Le magasin est ouvert tous les jours sauf le dimanche.
The shop is open every day except Sunday.

Il est rentré vers huit heures.
He came home at about eight o'clock.

✓ Maximise Your Marks

The French for 'a week' is **une semaine** but you can also use **huit jours** ('eight days').

The French for 'two weeks' is **deux semaines** but you can also say **quinze jours** ('15 days'). The French for 'a fortnight' is **une quinzaine**.

With dates, **à partir de** means 'from' and **jusqu'à** means 'until'. For example:
- **Je vais rester en France (à partir) du deux jusqu'au dix août.**
  I'm going to stay in France from the 2nd to the 10th of August.

❓ Test Yourself

What do these mean in English?
1. **J'aime me reposer dans le jardin.**
2. **Je n'aime pas aller en Espagne. C'est trop loin.**

How do you say these in French?
3. I went to Portugal on holiday.
4. I like doing winter sports.

⭐ Stretch Yourself

1. Say or write in French: 'I love Italy. I'm going there in May.'

2. Say or write in French: 'The cinema is expensive but we go there twice a month.'

Getting Around

Directions

Pardon, Madame	Excuse me, madam	**Prenez la première à gauche**	Take the first left
Excusez-moi, Monsieur	Excuse me, sir	**Prenez la deuxième à droite**	Take the second right
Pour aller au centre-ville?	How do I get to the town centre?	**Traversez la rue/ le pont**	Cross the street/bridge
Il y a une banque près d'ici?	Is there a bank near here?	**Allez jusqu'aux feux**	Go to the traffic lights
Où est le café le plus proche?	Where's the nearest café?	**Au coin de la rue**	At the corner of the street
Tournez à gauche/ droite	Turn left/right	**Au carrefour**	At the crossroads
Continuez tout droit	Go straight on	**Au rond-point**	At the roundabout

Planes, Trains, Buses and Cars

un aéroport	airport	**stationner**	to park
un avion	plane	**le volant**	steering wheel
un vol	flight	**un bouchon**	a traffic jam/hold-up
arrivées	arrivals	**des travaux**	roadworks
départs	departures		
la douane	customs	**la gare**	(train) station
le passeport	passport	**une station de métro**	underground station
les assurances	insurance (policy)	**l'entrée**	entrance
à l'heure	on time	**la sortie**	exit
en avance	early	**la sortie de secours**	emergency exit
en retard	late	**les renseignements**	information
		un horaire	timetable
une voiture/auto	car	**le guichet**	ticket office
l'autoroute (f.)	motorway	**un aller simple/ un billet simple**	single ticket
le parking	car park		
un piéton	pedestrian	**un aller-retour**	return ticket
une station-service	petrol station	**un carnet**	book of 10 tickets
une carte	map	**composter**	to punch/validate your ticket
un automobiliste	motorist		
l'essence (f.)	petrol	**une valise**	suitcase
le gazole	diesel	**des bagages**	luggage
le moteur	engine	**la consigne manuelle / automatique**	left luggage office/ lockers
le pare-brise	windscreen		
le péage	toll booth	**la salle d'attente**	waiting room
le permis de conduire	driving licence		
		un tramway	a tram
le pneu (crevé)	(flat) tyre	**un autobus**	a bus
la roue	wheel	**un ticket**	a bus ticket
		un conducteur	a driver

Travel Phrases

Les freins ne marchent pas.
The brakes aren't working.

Ma voiture est tombée en panne.
My car has broken down.

Je voudrais un aller simple pour Paris.
I'd like a single ticket to Paris.

Je voudrais voyager en deuxième classe.
I'd like to travel second class.

Je veux réserver une place.
I want to reserve a seat.

À quelle heure part le prochain train pour Bordeaux?
What time does the next train for Bordeaux leave?

Le train part de quel quai?
Which platform does the train leave from?

À quelle heure arrive le train?
What time does the train arrive?

C'est direct ou est-ce qu'il faut changer?
Is it direct or do I have to change?

On peut prendre la correspondance à Toulouse.
You can change in Toulouse.

Quel bus va au centre-ville? C'est quelle ligne?
Which bus goes to the town centre? What number is it?

Où est l'arrêt le plus proche?
Where's the nearest bus stop?

✓ Maximise Your Marks

Take care when talking about different ways of travelling. In English we usually say 'by' a means of transport ('by bus', 'by car' – but we say 'on foot'). In French, this can vary:
en autobus (by bus); **en voiture** (by car), **en avion** (by plane); **à pied** (on foot), **à vélo** (by bike); **par le train** (by train).

Build Your Skills: The Imperative

To give instructions and orders, you need to use a form of the verb known as the imperative.

If you are addressing a person with **tu**, use the **tu** form of the present tense of the verb, but without **tu**. With **–er** verbs you must also take off the **–s**. For example:
- **Prends la première à droite.**
  Take the first on the right.
- **Continue tout droit.** Go straight on.

If you are addressing a person/people with **vous**, use the **vous** form of the present tense, but without the **vous**. For example:
- **Mangez bien!** Eat well!
- **Continuez à travailler.** Carry on working.

The **nous** form of the present tense without the **nous** means 'let's' do something. For example:
- **Jouons au tennis.** Let's play tennis.

If you want to tell someone not to do something, put **ne...pas** around the verb. For example:
- **Ne parle pas.** Don't talk.
- **Ne parlez pas la bouche pleine.**
  Don't talk with your mouth full.

? Test Yourself

What do these mean in English?
1. **Tournez à gauche aux feux.**
2. **Je n'aime pas voyager en voiture, c'est fatigant.**

How do you say these in French?
3. I'd like a return ticket to Nice.
4. My car broke down on the motorway.

★ Stretch Yourself

1. Say or write in French: 'Don't watch TV. Let's go for a walk.'
2. Say or write in French: 'Change in Bordeaux and don't forget to phone me.'

Holiday Activities

My Favourite Activity

Je bronze	I sunbathe
Je me repose	I rest
Je nage	I swim
Je visite	I visit
Je fais du lèche-vitrine	I window-shop
Je fais de la voile/ de la planche à voile	I sail/windsurf
Je loue	I hire/rent
J'écris des cartes postales	I write postcards

Tous les ans, nous partons en France où mes parents louent un gîte à la campagne.
Every year we go to France where my parents rent a cottage in the country.

En vacances, j'oublie tout. Je bronze à la plage, je nage dans la mer et je visite des monuments historiques.
On holiday, I forget everything. I sunbathe on the beach, swim in the sea and visit historic monuments.

Cette année, en février, je pars dans les Alpes avec mon école pour faire des sports d'hiver. J'adore le ski.
This year in February, I'm setting off to the Alps with my school to do winter sports. I love skiing.

Last Year's Holiday

Où êtes-vous parti(e) en vacances cet été?
Where did you go on holiday this summer?

Je suis parti(e) en Bretagne en France.
I went to Brittany in France.

Quand? When?

J'y suis allé(e) au mois de juillet.
I went there in July.

Avec qui? Who with?

J'y suis allé(e) avec mes copains.
I went with my friends.

Pendant combien de temps?
For how long?

J'y ai passé quinze jours.
I spent two weeks there.

Comment avez-vous voyagé?
How did you travel?

Nous avons pris le bateau.
We took the boat.

✓ Maximise Your Marks

It can be impressive if you can use a past *and* a future tense in the same sentence. For example:

- **En mai je suis partie en France mais la semaine prochaine j'irai en Italie.**
  In May I went to France but next week I'll go to Italy.

My Ideal Holiday

Comment sont tes vacances idéales?
What's your ideal holiday?

Je voudrais partir aux États-Unis.
I'd like to go to the USA.

Je veux y passer un mois.
I want to spend a month there.

Nous voyagerons en avion et logerons dans un grand hôtel de luxe.
We'll travel by plane and stay in a big, luxurious hotel.

J'ai envie de faire du shopping dans les grands magasins à New York.
I want to go shopping in the department stores in New York.

J'irai avec mes copains parce que c'est plus amusant et j'aurai plus de liberté.
I'll go with my friends because it's more enjoyable and I'll have more freedom.

Build Your Skills: Saying Before and After Doing Something

To say 'before' is easy in French. Use **avant** (before) + **de** + the infinitive. For example:
- avant de **manger** before eating
- avant de **partir** before setting off

To say 'after' is a little more complicated. Use **après** (after) + **avoir** or **être** + the past participle. For example:
- après avoir **mangé** after eating
- après être **parti** after setting off

Note that agreements are needed for **être** verbs. Reflexive verbs all take **être** and need the extra pronoun. For example:

- **Après m'être levé, j'ai pris le petit déjeuner.**
  After getting up, I had breakfast.

- **Après s'être douchée, elle s'est habillée.**
  After having a shower, she got dressed.

Avant d'arriver, **j'ai mis mes lunettes de soleil.**
Before arriving, I put on my sunglasses.

Avant de bronzer, **j'ai mis mon maillot de bain.**
Before sunbathing, I put on my swimming costume.

Après avoir nagé, **j'ai bronzé près de la piscine.**
After swimming, I sunbathed beside the pool.

Après être arrivées, **les filles sont allées à l'hôtel.**
After arriving, the girls went to the hotel.

❓ Test Yourself

What do these mean in English?
1. **En vacances je veux simplement me relaxer.**
2. **J'ai bronzé, et puis j'ai nagé dans la mer.**

How do you say these in French?
3. I'd like to spend three weeks in Spain.
4. My friend loves shopping but I like visiting monuments.

★ Stretch Yourself

1. Say or write in French:
   before eating   after drinking
   before seeing   after falling

2. Say or write in French: 'After arriving at the beach, she swam in the sea before sunbathing.'

Accommodation

At the Hotel

le logement	accommodation
l'accueil	reception
la baignoire	bath
un balcon	balcony
une clé	key
le drap	sheet
un escalier	stairs
un lavabo	washbasin
un lit	bed
un grand lit	double bed
la note	the bill
le robinet	tap
la salle de bains	bathroom
un sèche-cheveux	hair dryer
du savon	soap
une serviette	towel

Je voudrais réserver une chambre pour deux nuits.
I'd like to reserve a room for two nights.

Je voudrais une chambre avec douche et une vue sur la mer.
I'd like a room with a shower and a sea view.

J'ai réservé une chambre pour deux personnes au nom de Francis.
I've booked a room for two people in the name of Francis.

À quelle heure est le petit déjeuner? C'est compris?
What time is breakfast? Is it included?

Notre télé ne marche pas et il n'y a pas de serviettes dans la salle de bains.
Our TV doesn't work and there are no towels in the bathroom.

Pouvez-vous me réveiller à sept heures demain matin?
Can you wake me at 7 tomorrow morning?

Ma chambre est au troisième étage.
My room's on the third floor.

Il faut prendre l'ascenseur.
I/you have to take the lift.

Le petit déjeuner est servi entre sept heures et dix heures dans la salle à manger qui se trouve au rez-de-chaussée.
Breakfast is served between 7 and 10 a.m. in the dining room, which is situated on the ground floor.

J'aime loger dans un hôtel parce que c'est plus confortable.
I like staying in a hotel because it's more comfortable.

Camping

la tente	tent
le bloc sanitaire	washroom
l'eau potable	drinking water
l'emplacement	pitch
le gaz	gas
une machine à laver	washing machine
des plats à emporter	takeaway food
une poubelle	bin
un sac de couchage	sleeping bag
la salle de jeux	games room

Avez-vous de la place pour une caravane? C'est combien par nuit?
Have you space for a caravan? How much is it per night?

On peut louer des vélos?
Can we hire bikes?

Le terrain est inondé. Il n'y a pas d'électricité.
The ground is flooded. There's no electricity.

Il n'y a pas d'eau chaude. Les douches sont froides.
There's no hot water. The showers are cold.

J'aime faire du camping parce que c'est moins cher et on a plus de liberté.
I like camping because it's cheaper and you've got more freedom.

Mais ce n'est pas agréable quand il pleut.
But it's not pleasant when it rains.

The Wider World

Asking Questions

After a question word (an interrogative), you often invert the verb (i.e. change its position) as in the English 'How are you?', rather than 'How you are?'

This sometimes gets tricky in French. Questions like 'What time is breakfast?' or 'Where is my room?' are easy: **À quelle heure est le petit déjeuner? Où est ma chambre?** But look at this example:
* What time does Marie get up?
  À quelle heure Marie se lève-t-elle?

You can avoid this tricky inversion by using **est-ce que**. This keeps the normal word order. So the question becomes:
* **À quelle heure est-ce que Marie se lève?**
  What time does Marie get up?

Other examples include:
* **Quand est-ce que vous partez?**
  When are you leaving?
* **Pourquoi est-ce que vous êtes arrivés en retard?**
  Why did you arrive late?

Build Your Skills: Problems

J'ai perdu...	I've lost...
On m'a volé...	I've had...stolen
Je l'ai laissé(e)...	I left it...
C'était...	It was...

le bureau des objets trouvés	lost property
mon appareil (photo)	my camera
mon portefeuille	my wallet
mon porte-monnaie	my purse
mon sac à main	my handbag
mon parapluie	my umbrella
un accident de la route	road accident
un pneu crevé	flat tyre
tomber en panne	to breakdown
heurter	to collide/to hit
renverser	to knock down
blessé	hurt/injured
un piéton	pedestrian
un conducteur	driver
un camion	lorry/truck

Hier j'ai perdu mon portefeuille dans la rue. Il est en cuir brun et il y avait deux cents euros dedans.
Yesterday I lost my wallet in the street. It's made of brown leather and it had 200 euros inside.

J'ai vu un accident ce matin. Une voiture a heurté un vélo et le cycliste est tombé.
I saw an accident this morning. A car hit a bike and the cyclist fell off.

Le conducteur n'était pas blessé mais le cycliste s'est cassé la jambe.
The driver wasn't hurt but the cyclist broke his leg.

✓ Maximise Your Marks

Always remember to give as many opinions as you can. So even when you are stating a fact you can always add an extra personal opinion:
* **J'ai logé dans une villa. C'était très jolie.**
  I stayed in a villa. It was very pretty.

? Test Yourself

What do these mean in English?
1. **Une chambre pour une personne avec salle de bains.**
2. **Je voudrais rester deux nuits.**

How do you say these in French?
3. The showers don't work
4. What time is lunch?

★ Stretch Yourself

1. Say or write in French: 'I broke my leg when I hit a tree.'
2. Say or write in French: 'I had my purse stolen in the car park.'

The Weather

Weather Expressions

une averse	shower
le brouillard	fog
la brume	mist
la chaleur	heat
le climat	climate
couvert	cloudy
un degré	degree
doux	mild
un éclair	lightning
une éclaircie	sunny period
ensoleillé	sunny
la glace	ice
humide	damp
mouillé	wet
un nuage	cloud
nuageux	cloudy
l'ombre	shade
un orage	thunderstorm
orageux	stormy/thundery
la pluie	rain
sec	dry
la température	temperature
une tempête	storm
le temps	weather
le tonnerre	thunder
trempé	soaked
Le soleil brille	The sun is shining
Il fait du soleil	It's sunny
Il gèle	It's freezing
Il neige	It's snowing
Il pleut	It's raining
Il fait beau	It's fine
Il fait mauvais	It's bad weather
Il fait froid	It's cold
Il fait chaud	It's hot
Il y a du vent	It's windy
Le ciel est bleu	The sky is blue

💡 Boost Your Memory

Try putting weather expressions to music. This song is to the tune of 'Here we go':

Il fait beau, il fait beau, il fait beau,
Il fait chaud, il fait chaud, il fait chaud,
Il fait froid, il fait froid, il fait froid,
Il pleut et il neige.

Adverbs

To form most adverbs, you take the feminine form of the adjective and add the ending **–ment**.

For example, the feminine form of **lent** (meaning 'slow') is **lente**. So the adverb is **lentement** (meaning 'slowly').

La température augmente très lentement.
The temperature's rising very slowly.

Malheureusement, il pleut.
Unfortunately, it's raining.

Le ciel était complètement couvert.
The sky was completely covered in cloud.

Vraiment (meaning 'really'/'truly') is an exception. It does not use the feminine form of **vrai**:
- **Il fait vraiment froid.** It is really cold.

Note also that the adverbs **vite** (quickly) and **soudain** (suddenly) do not obey this rule.

Note too adjectives like **fréquent** and **récent**. The adverbs are **fréquemment** and **récemment**.

Dans le nord, il pleut fréquemment.
In the north, it frequently rains.

Il a beaucoup neigé récemment.
It has snowed a
lot recently.

✓ Maximise Your Marks

Most people tend to concentrate on learning nouns and verbs. Make sure you also revise a stock of useful adjectives and adverbs which can be used in most contexts.

Useful adjectives include **joli**, **excellent**, **amusant** and **content**.

Useful adverbs are **soudain**, **lentement**, **vite** and **heureusement**.

Weather Forecasts

Voici la météo pour demain.
Here is the weather forecast for tomorrow.

Demain, il fera beau dans le nord. Il y aura de belles éclaircies, mais dans l'ouest il y aura du vent et il y aura des averses.
Tomorrow, it will be fine in the north. There will be some lovely sunny spells, but in the west it will be windy with showers.

Dans l'est, il fera assez froid avec un risque de pluie. Dans le sud, il fera très chaud mais il y aura peut-être des orages le soir.
In the east it will be quite cold with the risk of rain. In the south it will be very hot, but there will perhaps be thunderstorms in the evening.

? Test Yourself

What do these mean in English?
1 **Il y a du brouillard dans le nord-ouest de la France.**
2 **Soudain, il a commencé à pleuvoir. Heureusement, il a fait chaud.**

How do you say these in French?
3 The sky is really grey.
4 It will be extremely cold next week.

★ Stretch Yourself

1 Say or write in French: 'It was snowing when I left the house.'

2 Put the verb in brackets in the correct tense, perfect or imperfect.
   Je (bronzer) quand il (commencer) à pleuvoir. Il (faire) si froid qu'elle (mettre) un pull-over.

Build Your Skills: Perfect or Imperfect?

To say what the weather was like, you normally use the imperfect tense. For example:

Il pleuvait.	It was raining.
Il faisait beau.	It was fine.
Il y avait de la neige.	There was snow.
Le soleil brillait.	The sun was shining.

However, if you want to refer to a specific, limited time, then you need to use the perfect tense. For example:

Hier soir, il y a eu un orage.
Last night, there was a thunderstorm. (The thunderstorm might have started quite suddenly.)

Il y a eu du brouillard ce matin.
It was foggy this morning. (Here we have reference to a specific time – this morning. The fog has gone now.)

Il a plu pendant une heure.
It rained for an hour. (In this example, there is a specific amount of time stated. It rained for one hour only, then stopped.)

In many cases, you can start a sentence by using the imperfect tense to set the scene and then use the perfect once you start to narrate events.

Mardi dernier il pleuvait à verse, donc je suis resté à la maison.
Last Tuesday it was pouring down, so I stayed at home.

Il faisait tellement chaud que j'ai décidé de bronzer dans le jardin.
It was so hot that I decided to sunbathe in the garden.

Note these two expressions:
Un jour qu'il faisait beau, j'ai joué au tennis.
One day when it was fine, I played tennis.

Le jour où il faisait froid, j'ai fait du shopping.
The day when it was cold, I went shopping.

Life in Other Countries

Daily Life

French is spoken in many countries other than France. This includes European countries such as Belgium but also parts of Canada. In the Caribbean, the islands of Martinique and Guadeloupe are part of France. Many countries in Africa which are former colonies of France are also French speaking. In exam papers, questions are sometimes set on life in these countries.

J'habite au Togo en Afrique. I live in Togo in Africa.

Je me lève à cinq heures du matin pour prendre le car de ramassage scolaire.
I get up at 5 a.m. to catch the school bus.

Les cours commencent à 7h30. Il y a une cinquantaine d'élèves dans ma classe.
Lessons start at 7.30 a.m. There are about 50 pupils in my class.

Les cours finissent à midi et il n'y a pas de cantine scolaire, donc nous rentrons tous à la maison.
Lessons end at midday and there's no school canteen, so we all go home.

Il n'y a pas de cours l'après-midi parce qu'il fait trop chaud pour travailler.
There are no lessons in the afternoon because it's too hot to work.

En Martinique, les filles portent des robes en coton.
In Martinique, the girls wear cotton dresses.

D'habitude, on porte des bijoux comme des boucles d'oreille et un collier.
Usually, they wear jewellery, such as earrings and a necklace.

On met généralement un chapeau coloré.
They normally put on a colourful hat.

On porte le costume traditionnel pendant le carnaval.
Traditional costume is worn during the carnival.

Au Sénégal, les maisons ont souvent un seul étage.
In Senegal, houses often have only one floor.

On fait la cuisine dehors parce qu'il fait si chaud.
Cooking is done outside because it's so hot.

À la campagne, on élève quelquefois des animaux comme des moutons ou des chèvres dans le jardin.
In the countryside, people sometimes keep animals like sheep or goats in the garden.

Food in Other Countries

l'alimentation	food
la cuisine	cooking
le plat	dish
la spécialité	speciality
des ingrédients	ingredients
Ça se mange avec…	It's eaten with…
C'est fait avec…	It's made with…
épicé / piquant	spicy
doux	mild / sweet

Le couscous est une spécialité de l'Afrique du Nord.
Couscous is a speciality of North Africa.

C'est fait avec de la viande (souvent de l'agneau), des légumes, des oignons, des tomates et des épices.
It's made with meat (often lamb), vegetables, onions, tomatoes and spices.

Ça se mange avec une tasse de thé à la menthe.
It's eaten with mint tea.

Build Your Skills: The Pluperfect Tense

When you want to say what *had* happened before something else in the past, you need to use the pluperfect tense. It is formed by using the imperfect tense of **avoir** or **être** with the past participle. For example:

- **Je suis arrivé à l'aéroport mais** j'avais oublié **mon passeport.**

  I arrived at the airport (perfect tense) but I had forgotten (pluperfect) my passport.

Here is the pluperfect form of the verb **manger** in full:

J'avais mangé	I had eaten
Tu avais mangé	You had eaten
Il/Elle avait mangé	He/She had eaten
Nous avions mangé	We had eaten
Vous aviez mangé	You had eaten
Ils/Elles avaient mangé	They had eaten

Quand je suis rentré, ils avaient **déjà** mangé **les chocolats.**

When I got home, they had already eaten the chocolates.

There are of course some verbs such as **aller**, **arriver**, **rester** and **partir** which take **être** instead of **avoir**. Here is the pluperfect form of **partir** in full:

J'étais parti(e)	I had left
Tu étais parti(e)	You had left
Il était parti	He had left
Elle était partie	She had left
Nous étions parti(e)s	We had left
Vous étiez parti(e)(s)	You had left
Ils étaient partis	They had left (m.)
Elles étaient parties	They had left (f.)

Il était parti **sans moi.**
He had left without me.

Note how the pluperfect is used in the following sentences:

Dans la Creuse, au centre de la France, je suis allé à un festival qui s'appelle la Saint-Cochon.
In the Creuse in central France I went to a festival called la Saint-Cochon.

À la fin de la soirée, j'étais fatigué. On avait dansé, **on** avait chanté **et on** avait joué **aux jeux avec les enfants.**
At the end of the evening I was tired. We had danced, sung and played games with the children.

J'ai mangé des saucisses de porc. Les habitants du village avaient préparé **les saucisses la veille.**
I ate pork sausages. The inhabitants of the village had made the sausages the day before.

✓ Maximise Your Marks

Using the pluperfect is really impressive in written work at GCSE. You could bring it in naturally by using a normal perfect tense and then saying what had happened previously.

- **J'ai regardé un film mais je l'avais déjà vu.**
  I watched a film but I had already seen it.

- **Je suis arrivé à la gare mais le train était déjà parti.**
  I arrived at the station but the train had already gone.

? Test Yourself

What do these mean in English?
1. **Le costume traditionnel est joli.**
2. **La spécialité de la région est délicieuse.**

How do you say these in French?
3. She left without him.
4. The girls wear traditional jewellery.

★ Stretch Yourself

1. Put these verbs in the pluperfect tense (**elle** form):
   jouer arriver boire

2. Say or write in French: 'When he arrived in the village, the festival had already started.'

The Environment

Talking About Your Local Environment

l'environnement (m.)	environment
un arbre	tree
bruyant	noisy
calme	calm
un champ	field
la colline	hill
un espace vert	green belt/green space
une ferme	farm
une fleur	flower
la fumée	smoke
un incendie	fire
la lumière	light
un quartier	area (of a town)
une rivière	river
le trottoir	pavement
une usine	factory
la circulation	traffic
les déchets	waste
la paix	peace
les papiers/détritus	litter
pollué	polluted
propre	clean
une poubelle	bin
sale	dirty

Mon village est calme et tranquille. Il y a beaucoup de fleurs et d'arbres. L'air est propre.
My village is calm and quiet. There are lots of flowers and trees. The air is clean.

Ma ville est sale et industrielle. Il y a beaucoup d'usines et de circulation. Et la rivière devient polluée à cause des déchets.
My town is dirty and industrial. There are a lot of factories and traffic. And the river gets polluted because of waste.

Ma ville est jolie. Mais le week-end des touristes laissent tomber des papiers par terre.
My town is pretty. But at the weekend tourists drop litter.

What I Do to Protect the Environment

Je ferme le robinet pour économiser de l'eau quand je me brosse les dents.
I turn off the tap to save water when brushing my teeth.

J'éteins toutes les lumières quand je sors d'une pièce.
I switch off all the lights when I leave a room.

Je recycle le verre, le carton, le plastique et les boîtes.
I recycle glass, cardboard, plastic and tins.

Au supermarché, il y a trop d'emballages. Je n'utilise plus de sacs en plastique.
At the supermarket there is too much packaging. I don't use plastic bags any more.

Dans ma ville, il y a un centre de recyclage. Nous avons des poubelles spéciales pour recycler les journaux et les bouteilles.
In my town, there is a recycling centre. We have special bins for recycling newspapers and bottles.

Je cultive des fruits et des légumes dans le jardin et je ne jette pas les déchets que je peux utiliser pour faire du compost.
I grow fruit and vegetables in the garden and I don't throw away waste that I can use to make compost.

Problems and Solutions

Il y a trop de voitures. Les gaz d'échappement polluent l'air.
There are too many cars. Exhaust fumes pollute the air.

Il faut encourager les gens à ne pas prendre leurs voitures. On peut aller au travail à pied.
We must encourage people to stop using their cars. You can walk to work.

Aux heures d'affluence, il y a beaucoup d'embouteillages.
At rush hour there are a lot of traffic jams.

Il faut développer les transports en commun parce que l'air est pollué.
We must develop public transport because the air is polluted.

Il faut créer des zones piétonnes et des pistes cyclables.
We must create pedestrian zones and cycle lanes.

Dans certaines villes, les voitures sont interdites au centre-ville. Ainsi, l'air est plus propre et la pollution est réduite.
In some towns, cars are not allowed in the centre. Therefore, the air is cleaner and pollution is reduced.

? Test Yourself

What do these mean in English?
1. **Ma ville est polluée à cause de la circulation.**
2. **Il faut recycler le verre et le papier.**

How do you say these in French?
3. I go to school on foot.
4. The pupils go to school by bus.

★ Stretch Yourself

1. Make these sentences passive:
   Maman écrira une lettre.
   Sophie a fait une tarte.

2. Say or write in French: 'In my town, paper is recycled by everyone.'

Build Your Skills: The Passive

Verbs usually have an active subject.
For example, in the sentence 'The dog bit the man', the dog is the subject of the verb; the dog is the one that is actively doing something (the biting). The sentence can be rearranged as 'The man was bitten (by the dog)' – it is now a passive sentence; the subject is now the man but the man is not doing anything active. Here is another example:

I wrote the poem. (active)
The poem was written (by me). (passive)

As in English, you form the passive in French by using the verb **être** (to be) in the correct tense, followed by the past participle.
For example:

La circulation a été réduite.
Traffic has been reduced.

Les sacs seront réutilisés.
The bags will be re-used.

La pollution est causée **par les gaz d'échappement.**
Pollution is caused by exhaust fumes.

Note that the past participle is treated as an adjective and has to agree with the first noun. For example, **la pollution** is feminine so you need **–e** on the past participle **causée**. **Les sacs** are masculine plural and so you add **–s** to the past participle **réutilisés**.

⚲ Boost Your Memory

Some exam questions ask you to identify speakers' opinions, and to say if they have positive, negative or mixed views on a topic.

If the speaker has mixed views, often you will hear them use an expression that indicates they have both positive and negative views. An obvious example is **mais** (but).

In your revision, make sure you also note and revise words like **cependant** (however), **pourtant** (yet), **tandis que** (whereas), **d'autre part** (on the other hand).

Global Issues

Endangered Species

les espèces menacées	endangered species
la baleine	whale
le blaireau	badger
la chauve-souris	bat
le dauphin	dolphin
un éléphant	elephant
le guépard	cheetah
les oiseaux	birds
un ours	bear
le panda	panda
le phoque	seal
les poissons	fish
le renard	fox
le rhinocéros	rhino
le tigre	tiger
le singe	monkey

Il faut protéger les espèces menacées.
We should protect endangered/threatened species.

Le tigre est en danger de disparaître.
The tiger is in danger of disappearing.

Les ours polaires sont menacés d'extinction.
Polar bears are threatened with extinction.

Il faut sauver les baleines et interdire la chasse.
We should save whales and ban hunting.

Some Useful Verbs

améliorer	to improve
augmenter	to increase
conserver	to conserve / save
créer	to create
détruire	to destroy
endommager	to damage
fournir	to provide
gaspiller	to waste
nettoyer	to clean

Issues Affecting Our Planet

la consommation	consumption
le charbon	coal
la couche d'ozone	ozone layer
le déboisement	deforestation
les déchets	waste
l'effet de serre	the greenhouse effect
l'essence	petrol
le gaz carbonique	carbon gas
le monde	the world
mondial	worldwide
la Terre	the Earth
les ordures	rubbish
le pétrole	crude oil
la pluie acide	acid rain
sans plomb	unleaded
les ressources	resources
surpeuplé	overpopulated
un tremblement de terre	earthquake
le trou	hole
la vague	wave
l'énergie renouvelable	renewable energy
l'énergie nucléaire	nuclear energy
l'énergie solaire	solar power
l'énergie éolienne	wind power
la guerre	war
le terrorisme	terrorism
la pauvreté	poverty
la famine	famine
l'insécurité	crime/insecurity

En Afrique les gens meurent de faim.
In Africa people are dying of hunger.

On pourrait supprimer les dettes des pays en voie de développement pour réduire la pauvreté.
We could cancel the debts of the developing countries to reduce poverty.

Je me sens concerné par le réchauffement de la terre.
I am concerned by global warming.

Build Your Skills: The Conditional Tense

We use the conditional tense when we want to say what *would* happen. You have already used the conditional tense of **vouloir** in the form **je voudrais** (I would like).

To form the conditional tense, you use the same form of the verb as the future tense (usually the infinitive) and then add exactly the same endings as the imperfect tense.

Here is a regular verb in the conditional tense – the verb **jouer** in the infinitive form with the imperfect endings:

Je jouerais	I would play
Tu jouerais	You would play
Il/Elle jouerait	He/She would play
Nous jouerions	We would play
Vous joueriez	You would play
Ils/Elles joueraient	They would play

Now here is an irregular verb. The verb **faire** uses the form **fer–** in the future, so the conditional form of the verb is as follows:

Je ferais	I would do, would make
Tu ferais	You would do, would make
Il/Elle ferait	He/She would do, would make
Nous ferions	We would do, would make
Vous feriez	You would do, would make
Ils/Elles feraient	They would do, would make

To impress examiners you can use the conditional tense in structures using the word **si** (if). **Si** changes to **s'** before **il**. Immediately after **si**, you use the imperfect tense, but then you need to use the conditional tense in the main clause:

Si j'étais **riche, j'**irais **en Australie.**
If I was rich, I would go to Australia.

Si on faisait **des efforts, on** réduirait **la pollution.**
If we made the effort (imperfect), we would reduce pollution (conditional).

Si le gouvernment interdisait **les voitures au centre-ville, il** y aurait **moins de pollution.**
If the government banned cars in the town centre, there would be less pollution.

Si on faisait **plus d'efforts, on** supprimerait **les sacs en plastique.**
If we made more effort, we would abolish plastic bags.

Si les transports en commun étaient **meilleurs, on ne** construirait **pas de nouvelles routes.**
If public transport was better, we wouldn't build new roads.

⚡ Boost Your Memory

If you would like to use the conditional tense in your work but find it tricky, learn a set expression that you can adapt for most topics, for example **Si c'était possible, je voudrais...** (If it was possible, I would...):

- **Si c'était possible, je voudrais aider les pauvres.**
  If it was possible, I would like to help poor people.

Practise using this phrase in different contexts, for example:

- **Si c'était possible, je voudrais habiter dans une grande maison.**
- **Si c'était possible, je voudrais aller à l'université.**

❓ Test Yourself

What do these mean in English?
1. **Il faut sauver les pandas et les tigres.**
2. **Il est important de réduire le réchauffement de la terre.**

How do you say these in French?
3. I think that solar power is useful.
4. We must protect the planet.

⭐ Stretch Yourself

1. Say or write in French: 'If we wanted, we could protect threatened species.'
2. Say or write in French: 'If we did nothing, many animals would be threatened with extinction.'

Social Issues

Issues Affecting Society

les responsabilités	responsibilities
le sondage	survey
la manifestation	demonstration
la guerre	war
le travail bénévole	voluntary work
une organisation caritative	charity
le SIDA	AIDS
la pauvreté	poverty
pauvre	poor
le chômage	unemployment
les dettes	debts
les défavorisés	those less fortunate
les exclus	the excluded
l'égalité	equality
la famine	famine
les sans-abris	the homeless
un SDF (sans domicile fixe)	a homeless person
sans travail	unemployed
le racisme	racism

Chrétien	Christian
Musulman	Muslim
Juif	Jewish
la discrimination	discrimination
les immigrés	immigrants
les réfugiés	refugees
la couleur de la peau	skin colour
les droits	rights
la vérité	truth
l'insécurité	crime/insecurity
un malfaiteur	criminal
un voyou	thug
le vandalisme	vandalism
la violence	violence
le vol	theft
le voleur	thief

Il faut combattre la pauvreté.
It's necessary to/We must fight poverty.

Il faut protéger les droits de l'homme.
It's necessary to protect human rights.

Il faut promouvoir l'égalité des chances.
We must promote equal opportunities.

Tackling Social Issues

aider	to help
il s'agit de...	it's about...
agresser	to attack
battre	to beat
se battre avec	to fight with
cacher	to hide
combattre	to combat/fight
consacrer	to devote/commit
déranger	to disturb
éviter	to avoid
garder	to keep
lutter contre	to struggle/fight against
menacer	to threaten
plaindre	to pity/feel sorry for
se plaindre	to complain

protéger	to protect
protester	to protest
réaliser	to achieve

Tu veux aller à une manifestation pour protester contre la discrimination raciale?
Do you want to go to a demonstration to protest against racial discrimination?

Voulez-vous contribuer à une organisation caritative?
Do you want to contribute to a charity?

Je veux faire du travail bénévole.
I want to do some voluntary work.

Il faut lutter contre le racisme.
We must fight against racism.

Tackling Social Issues (cont.)

L'insécurité menace la société – il faut consacrer plus d'argent pour combattre le problème.
Crime threatens society – we must commit more money to fight this problem.

Je veux aider les sans-abris et j'ai l'intention de collecter de l'argent pour réaliser mon ambition.
I want to help the homeless and I intend to collect/raise money to achieve my ambition.

✓ Maximise Your Marks

It is vital to give plenty of opinions when talking or writing about an issue. Try, however, to vary the way you express your opinions. **Je pense que** (I think that) and **je crois que** (I believe that) are useful but also use **à mon avis** (in my opinion), **il me semble que** (it seems to me), **en ce qui me concerne** (as far as I'm concerned).

❓ Test Yourself

What do these mean in English?
1. **Je veux protester contre le chômage.**
2. **Tu veux participer à la manifestation contre la guerre?**

How do you say these in French?
3. I intend to do some voluntary work.
4. We need to combat discrimination.

⭐ Stretch Yourself

1. Write this sentence in French: 'It would be a good idea if one could use more renewable energy.'
2. Say or write in French: 'We should collect money in order to fight poverty.'

Build Your Skills: The Pronoun 'On'

The pronoun **on** (literally 'one') is often used in French when you are not referring to a specific person. It can be translated as 'you', 'we' or 'they'. It is followed by the same form of the verb as **il** and **elle**. For example:

- **On proteste contre la guerre.**
  They are protesting against the war.
- **On dit que la violence devient pire.**
  They (people) say that violence is getting worse.
- **Si on veut combattre la pauvreté, on peut faire du travail bénévole pour aider les pauvres.**
  If you want to fight poverty, you can do voluntary work to help poor people.

You already know how useful the conditional tense of the verb **vouloir** is (**je voudrais**). The verbs **pouvoir** and **devoir** are also very useful in the conditional tense when used with the pronoun **on**:

On **pourrait**   One/We could, might
On **devrait**   One/We should, ought

Ce serait une bonne idée si on pourrait aider les gens qui meurent de faim.
It would be a good idea if we could help people who are dying of hunger.

On pourrait développer des énergies renouvelables.
We could develop renewable energy.

On devrait faire plus d'efforts pour combattre la famine.
We should make more effort to combat famine.

On devrait utiliser les transports en commun.
We ought to use public transport.

The verbs **falloir** and **valoir** can also be used in the conditional tense but *not* with the pronoun **on**:

Il faudrait faire plus d'efforts.
We should make more effort.

Cela en vaudrait la peine.
It would be worthwhile.

Practice Questions

Complete these exam-style questions to test your skills and understanding. Check your answers on page 94. You may wish to answer these questions on a separate piece of paper.

The Wider World

Reading

1 Read the sentences below and match them to the descriptions that follow.

A **Quand il fait froid en hiver, je mets un pull-over au lieu d'utiliser le chauffage central.**

B **J'éteins toujours la lumière quand je quitte une pièce.**

C **Aujourd'hui, en France, seule une bouteille sur trois est recyclée. C'est une honte.**

D **Je recycle les journaux. Cela permet de sauver des forêts.**

E **Je ferme le robinet quand je me brosse les dents et je me douche au lieu de prendre un bain.**

F **J'achète toujours des biscuits emballés dans du carton, plutôt que dans du plastique.**

a) Saving electricity ☐ (1)   b) Saving water ☐ (1)

c) Recycling paper ☐ (1)   d) Too much packaging ☐ (1)

e) Avoiding using the central heating ☐ (1)   f) Recycling glass ☐ (1)

2 In the passage below, Florine talks about her holiday. Read the passage and answer the questions that follow in English.

> Il y a deux ans, je suis allée dans les Alpes pour faire du ski. Je suis partie en février et j'ai passé une semaine dans les Alpes françaises. J'ai voyagé par le train. C'était long et fatigant. J'ai logé dans une auberge de jeunesse. Pendant la journée, j'ai fait du ski ou j'ai fait des randonnées dans les montagnes. Le soir, je suis allée dans un bar où j'ai bu du vin et j'ai dansé. Il a fait très froid et il a beaucoup neigé.

a) Where did Florine go and why?

.... (2)

b) How long did she stay?

.... (1)

c) How did she get there?

.... (1)

d) What was her opinion of the journey?

.... (2)

e) Where did she stay?

.... (1)

f) What did she do in the evenings?

.... (3)

g) What was the weather like?

.... (2)

Speaking

3 You are to give an account of a holiday. Prepare to speak about each of the following points in French.

   a) Describe where you went and how you got there.

   b) Say where you stayed and what you did during your visit.

   c) Give your opinion of the visit.

   d) Say where you would like to go next year and why.

   (10)

Writing

4 You are writing about your plans to make your town more environmentally friendly. Write about each of the following in French.
- Say what you think are the main problems with your local environment.
- Describe what you intend to do to overcome these problems.
- Describe where you would like to live in the future.
- Give reasons why you want to live there.

(15)

How well did you do?

| 1–14 | Try again | 15–24 | Getting there | 25–34 | Good work | 35–43 | Excellent! |

Word Bank

Here are some additional items of vocabulary for each of the four topic areas.
These words are only likely to come up in higher tier listening and reading questions.

Lifestyle

une odeur	a smell	un jeu (de société)	(board)game
plein	full	un jouet	toy
tousser	to cough	la maison de la presse	newsagents
vivre	to live	mettre de l'argent de côté	to put money aside
à peine	scarcely	l'orchestre (m.)	stalls (at theatre or cinema)
à point	medium (steak)	la promotion	special offer
de l'ail	garlic	réduit	reduced
amer/amère	bitter	le rouge à lèvres	lipstick
avertir	to warn	taper	to type
bien cuit	well done (steak)		
le canard	duck	annuler	to cancel
un casse-croûte	snack	l'antenne (f.)	aerial
une casserole	a saucepan	une boîte aux lettres	electronic mail box
une côtelette	a chop	électronique	
une crevette	a prawn	un caméscope	camcorder
cru	raw	une capuche	a hoody
une dégustation	food tasting	le comptoir	counter
la douleur	pain	la console de jeu	games console
s'entraîner	to train	le courrier électronique	email
épais/épaisse	thick	déchirer	to tear
épuiser	to exhaust	dérouler vers le	to scroll up/down
la farine	flour	bas/haut	
le foie	liver	faire défiler	to scroll
gâcher	to spoil	deviner	to guess
un gigot d'agneau	leg of lamb	un distributeur automatique	cash dispenser
hors d'haleine	out of breath	effacer	to delete/erase
une huître	oyster	emballer	to wrap
ivre	drunk	un escalier roulant	escalator
les matières grasses	fat	être remboursé	to get money back
mener	to lead	feuilleter	to leaf through
une noix	nut	les fléchettes	darts
un ouvre-boîte	tin-opener	un fleuriste	florist
une piqûre	injection/sting	un genre	a type/a kind
un poumon	lung	imprimer	to print
renoncer	to give up	lancer	to throw
reprendre connaissance	to regain consciousness	lourd	heavy
respirer	to breathe	un magnétoscope	a video recorder
saignant	rare (steak)	marquer (un but)	to score (a goal)
salé	salty	en avoir marre	to be fed up
sauvegarder	to safeguard	la mi-temps	half-time
savoureux	tasty	les mots croisés	crossword
un tire-bouchon	corkscrew	la page d'accueil	homepage
une truite	trout	la plongée sous-marine	underwater diving
tuer	to kill	la prise	plug/socket
du vinaigre	vinegar	la réclame	advertisement/offer
		un réseau	network
une ceinture	belt	un tatouage	tattoo
un concours	competition	une tournée	a tour
démodé	old-fashioned	le traitement de texte	word processing
fan de	fan of		

The Wider World

se baigner	to swim
le bureau des renseignements	information office
un carnet	notebook
la demi-pension	half board
un drapeau	flag
la location de voitures	car hire
se mettre en route	to set off
la pension complète	full board
le pourboire	tip
le sable	sand
sens interdit	no entry
sens unique	one-way street
un couloir	corridor
une île	island
un immeuble	multi-storey building
un toit	roof
atterrir	to land
décoller	to take off
un casque	helmet
le chemin de fer	railway
la climatisation	air conditioning
la déviation	diversion
en provenance de	from (train's starting point)
la marée	tide
un niveau	a level
un panneau	a sign
un passage à niveau	level crossing
ralentir	to slow down
remarquer	to notice
une station balnéaire	seaside resort
une station de ski	ski resort
un tiroir	drawer
la Toussaint	All Saints' Day (1 November)
les libertés civiques	civil liberties
les droits de l'homme	human rights
empêcher	to prevent/stop
un enlèvement	kidnapping
exclus	excluded
une mosquée	mosque

School and Work

bien/mal équipé	well/badly equipped
un car de ramassage scolaire	school bus
la connaissance	knowledge
couramment	fluently
un diplôme	a qualification
doué	talented
la faculté	faculty/university
les incivilités	anti-social behaviour/rudeness
l'instruction religieuse	RE
les langues vivantes	modern foreign languages
une licence	a degree
mal équipé	badly equipped
la maternelle	nursery
redoubler	to repeat a school year
la rentrée	start of school year
la retenue	detention
un souci	a concern
surchargé	overcrowded
une tâche	a task
se taire	to be quiet
traduire	to translate
les affaires	business
un boulot	work/job (slang)
une carrière	career
discuter	to discuss
une foire-exposition	trade fair
licencier	to sack/lay off/make redundant
la loi	the law
une offre d'emploi	job offer
la retraite	retirement
un auteur	author/writer
un cadre	manager
un comptable	accountant
une femme de ménage	cleaner
un jardinier	gardener
un instituteur	primary school teacher (male)
une institutrice	primary school teacher (female)
le/la propriétaire	the owner
un routier	truck driver

Home Life

la carte d'identité	identity card
un lieu	a place
le voisin/la voisine	neighbour
un/une ado	teenager
un baiser	a kiss
des conseils	advice
coupable	guilty
de mauvaise humeur	in a bad mood
déçu	disappointed

l'ennui (m.)	trouble
une enquête	enquiry
envahir	to invade
l'espoir (m.)	hope
l'esprit	wit/mind
inconnu	unknown
reconnaissant	grateful
sans ressources	poor
un témoin	witness
un volet	a shutter

Communication Strategies

It is very important to concentrate on learning vocabulary and key language for each topic area. However, it is not possible to predict all the words you might meet in listening and reading tests or what words you might want to use in speaking and writing. It is therefore advisable to familiarise yourself with some key communication strategies. These will help you work out the meaning of unfamiliar words and broaden your vocabulary in order to make your speaking and writing more varied.

Visual and Verbal clues

When reading a text many clues can be found in the layout of the passage and any pictures or diagrams that go with it. Look carefully at the title, too, to get the gist of the passage.

You can also develop the skill of inferring the meaning of new words. For example:

Dans la forêt, il y avait beaucoup d'arbres. Sur la branche d'un chêne un oiseau chantait.

You might not know the meaning of the word **chêne**, but by looking at the context – the words **forêt**, **arbres**, **branche** and the fact that there is a bird singing on it – you could infer that it is a kind of tree. **Un chêne** is actually an oak tree.

Similarly, in the sentence **Sur la branche d'un arbre un moineau chantait**, you could probably work out that **un moineau** is a kind of bird. It is, in fact, a sparrow.

Faux Amis

There are many words which are the same in both French and English but you need to take care of the so-called **faux amis** (false friends), which can catch you out.

Travailler means 'to work' *not* to travel. ('To travel' is **voyager**.)

Une journée is 'a day' *not* a journey. ('A journey' is **un voyage**.)

Un car is 'a coach' *not* a car. ('A car' is **une voiture**.)

Sensible means 'sensitive' *not* sensible. ('Sensible' is **raisonnable** or **sensé**.)

Simplify

In speaking or writing, do not try to be too ambitious. If you are unsure of a word or phrase, try to find an alternative. If you want to express a future plan, but you are not certain you can form the future tense of the key verb, use **je vais** or **je voudrais** with the infinitive instead. The future tense of verbs such as **faire** and **voir** are quite hard. So instead of saying **je ferai du shopping samedi**, you could say **je vais faire du shopping samedi**. Instead of **je verrai le film la semaine prochaine**, you could say **je voudrais voir le film la semaine prochaine**.

Paraphrase

If you get stuck when thinking of a key word, paraphrase to avoid using that word.

For example, **célibataire** means 'single', but if you are not sure how to say it or spell it you could say **il n'est pas marié** instead.

You might want to say you like eating lamb (**l'agneau**) but if you forgot the word why not just say you like meat – **j'aime manger de la viande**?

Common Patterns

In French, certain words follow patterns which can give you a clue as to their meaning. Many shops end in **–erie**, such as **la boulangerie**, **la boucherie**, **la charcuterie**. You should be able to work out that **la parfumerie** is a perfume shop, and that **la poissonnerie** is a fishmonger's.

If a verb starts with **re–**, it often means to do something again. **Commencer** means 'to begin' and **recommencer** means 'to begin again'.

You should be able to work out adjectives ending in **–able** if you recognise the verbs they are formed from. **Mangeable** means 'eatable' and **lavable** means 'washable', for example.

Similarly, many nouns formed from verbs end in **–ion**. **Inventer** means 'to invent' and **une invention** is an invention. **Inviter** means 'to invite' and an invitation is **une invitation**.

Look out also for the following:

- Adverbs ending in **–ment** where in English we use '–ly': **généralement**, **complètement**, **finalement**.

- Adjectives ending in **–ant** where in English we use '–ing': **intéressant**, **fatigant**, **charmant**.

- Adjectives which end in **–eux** in French where in English we use '–ous': **délicieux**, **précieux**.

- Words which end in **–que** in French but '–c' or '–k' in English: **la musique**, **automatique**, **physique**.

- The **–eur** ending which can make a verb into a noun, e.g. **chanter – chanteur**, or make an adjective into a noun, e.g. **grand, grandeur**; **chaud, chaleur**.

- The **–ette** ending, meaning something is very small: **maison – maisonette**; **fille – fillette**.

- The **–aine** ending added to a number means 'about', so **vingt** is 20 but **une vingtaine** means 'about 20'. Note also **quinze – quinzaine**; **cent – centaine**.

- The **–té** ending added to an adjective can form a noun: **bon – bonté**; **beau – beauté**.

- **in** at the beginning of a word is often like 'un' in English: **actif – inactif**; **connu – inconnu**).

Cognates and Near-cognates

There are very many words which have the same form, and often the same meaning, in French and in English. These are known as 'cognates', e.g. innocent, justice, nation, international.

Then there are the so-called 'near-cognates': you can be expected to understand words which differ only slightly in their written form in French usually by the addition of an accent or extra letter or by the repetition of a letter, e.g. **création**, **hygiène**, **littérature**.

Here are some other near-cognates:

- Words where there is an **e** at the end of the French but no 'e' in the English: **branche**, **vaste**

- Words where there is an 'e' at the end of the English but no **e** in French: **futur**, **masculin**

- Words which end with **e**, **é** or **e** in French but with 'y' in English: **beauté**, **liberté**

- Words which end with **el** in French and with 'al' in English: **individuel**, **officiel**

- Verbs which have **–er** in the infinitive in French: **admirer**, **copier**, **cliquer**, **inspecter**

- Verbs which end with **–er** in French and with '–ate' in English: **cultiver**, **décorer**

- Words where there is a 'd' in English but not in French: **aventure**, **avantage**

- Words which end with **–f** in French and with '–ve' in English: **actif**, **adjectif**

- Words which end with **–e** or **–re** in French and with '–er' in English: **ministre**, **ordre**

- Words which have a circumflex accent in French and an 's' in English: **forêt**, **honnête**, **intérêt**

- Words where **é** or **es** in French is replaced by 's' in English: **espace**, **étable**, **école**.

Key Tenses

In speaking and writing, you cannot gain good marks unless you use at least two different tenses. Ideally, you should try to use past, present and future in every speaking and writing task you do.

Here is a reminder of some key verbs in all three time frames.

The Present Tense

Here are some regular **–er**, **–ir** and **–re** verbs, plus a reflexive verb. Spot the pattern in each group:

Verbe	jouer	finir	rendre	se coucher
	to play	to finish	to give back	to go to bed
Je	joue	finis	rends	me couche
Tu	joues	finis	rends	te couches
Il/Elle	joue	finit	rend	se couche
Nous	jouons	finissons	rendons	nous couchons
Vous	jouez	finissez	rendez	vous couchez
Ils/Elles	jouent	finissent	rendent	se couchent

Here are some very common irregular verbs, which need to be learned separately:

Verbe	avoir	être	aller	faire	prendre	vouloir	pouvoir	venir
	to have	to be	to go	to do	to take	to want	to be able	to come
Je/J'	ai	suis	vais	fais	prends	veux	peux	viens
Tu	as	es	vas	fais	prends	veux	peux	viens
Il/Elle	a	est	va	fait	prend	veut	peut	vient
Nous	avons	sommes	allons	faisons	prenons	voulons	pouvons	venons
Vous	avez	êtes	allez	faites	prenez	voulez	pouvez	venez
Ils/Elles	ont	sont	vont	font	prennent	veulent	peuvent	viennent

The Perfect Tense

The perfect tense is probably the most important tense you will use in your work and it is essential to get it right. You must know the present tense forms of the verbs **avoir** and **être** (page 12) and the past participle of the verbs you want to use.

Most verbs in the perfect tense are formed with **avoir** followed by the past participle of the

verb – e.g. **j'ai mangé**, which means 'I have eaten' or 'I ate'. The vast majority of verbs go like **manger**.

However, you need to know the verbs which use **être** rather than **avoir** (see page 42 for a list), and you also need to learn the past participles of irregular verbs.

The Perfect Tense (cont.)

When forming the perfect tense, remember that it is the **avoir** or **être** that you have to change to match the person doing the action:

Tu as bu le vin?	Did you drink the wine?
Elle a joué au tennis.	She played tennis.
Nous sommes partis en retard.	We set off late.
Ils ont vu le film.	They saw/have seen the film.

With verbs that take **avoir** the past participle does not change. But with **être** verbs, the past participle works like an adjective and agrees with the person or people doing the action: e.g. **elles sont parties** (they have left, they left).

Here are some useful verbs in the perfect tense, which you can use in most essays and speaking tasks:

Je suis allé(e)	I went
Je suis parti(e)	I set off
Je suis resté(e)	I stayed
J'ai visité	I visited
J'ai acheté	I bought
J'ai joué	I played
J'ai mangé	I ate
J'ai bu	I drank

Finally, note what happens to reflexive verbs in the perfect tense:

Je me suis bien amusé(e)   I had a good time

The Imperfect Tense

The imperfect tense is used for descriptions in the past, for incomplete actions or for what used to happen.

The imperfect is easy to form. Take the **nous** form of the present tense, remove the **–ons** and add these endings:

Je regardais la télé	I was watching TV
Tu regardais la télé	You were watching TV
Il/Elle regardait la télé	He/She was watching TV
Nous regardions la télé	We were watching TV
Vous regardiez la télé	You were watching TV
Ils/Elles regardaient la télé	They were watching TV

The only exception is the verb **être**, which goes **j'étais**, **tu étais**, **il était** and so on.

In the following sentence, the imperfect is used for an incomplete action:

Le voleur portait un masque et il avait un revolver à la main.
The thief was wearing a mask and had a revolver in his hand.

Here is an example of the imperfect to express what used to happen:

Quand j'étais petite, je jouais avec des poupées.
When I was little, I used to play with dolls.

The Future Tense

This tense is the equivalent of the English 'I will do' or 'I'll do'. In French, the future tense is formed from the infinitive (removing the final **–e** if necessary) and adding these endings:

Je prendrai	**Nous prendrons**
Tu prendras	**Vous prendrez**
Il/Elle prendra	**Ils/Elles prendront**

Some irregular verbs, although they always use the same endings, form the future with a special 'stem' and not the infinitive. Here are some common ones:

Je serai	I'll be
J'aurai	I'll have
Je ferai	I'll do/make
J'irai	I'll go
Je verrai	I'll see
Je viendrai	I'll come

À la Saint-Sylvestre, nous aurons une fête.
On New Year's Eve, we'll have a party.

✓ Maximise your marks

Always include all three of the following forms of **être** somewhere in your written work:

C'est = It is	→ **C'est amusant**
C'était = It was	→ **C'était super**
Ce sera = It will be	→ **Ce sera fantastique**

Answers

Guidance for the Speaking and Writing Answers to the Practice Questions

Speaking

Marks will be awarded as follows:

9–10 Marks
Very Good
This means you have covered all the points and given detailed answers, including plenty of relevant information. You have spoken clearly, and have included opinions and reasons for your opinions. You have used some longer sentences and you have used more than one tense.

7–8 Marks
Good
This means you have covered all the points but one of the points may not be as detailed as the others. You have given quite a lot of information clearly, and have included some opinions and reasons. You have used some longer sentences and you have used more than one tense.

5–6 Marks
Sufficient
This means you might not have covered one or two of the points but what you have said conveys some information and there are opinions expressed. Most of your sentences are quite short and your answer may not show much evidence of different tenses.

3–4 Marks
Limited
This means that you have spoken in brief sentences and included some simple opinions but your answer lacks detail and you have missed out some of the information you were asked to give. Your sentences are short and you have used only one tense.

1–2 Marks
Poor
This means that you could not really answer the question and that you gave very little information and expressed no opinions. All your sentences are short and in the same tense.

Writing

Marks will be awarded as follows:

13–15 Marks
Very Good
This means you have covered all the bullet points and given a detailed answer, including plenty of relevant information. You have written clearly, and have included opinions and reasons for your opinions. You have set out your work in a logical and clear structure. You have used some longer sentences and you have used more than one tense.

10–12 Marks
Good
This means you have covered all the bullet points but one of the points may not be as detailed as the others. You have given quite a lot of information clearly, and have included some opinions and reasons. There are some longer sentences and you have used more than one tense.

7–9 Marks
Sufficient
This means you might not have covered one or two of the bullet points but what you have written conveys some information and there are opinions expressed. Most of your sentences are quite short and your answer may not show much evidence of different tenses.

4–6 Marks
Limited
This means that you have written some brief sentences and included some simple opinions but your answer lacks detail and you have missed out some of the information you were asked to give. Your sentences are short and you have used only one tense.

1–3 Marks
Poor
This means that you could not really answer the question and that you have given very little information and expressed no opinions. All your sentences are short and in the same tense.

Introduction

Pages 6–7 Basic Phrases and Expressions
Test Yourself Answers
1. le premier janvier
2. douze, vingt-cinq, quarante-deux, soixante-deux, soixante-douze, cent un

Stretch Yourself Answers
1. a) Bonne nuit! b) Bonne chance! c) Félicitations!

Pages 8–9
Test Yourself Answers
1. Jeudi
2. Il est dix-huit heures trente. Il est huit heures quinze.

Stretch Yourself Answers
1. Où est ta maison?
2. J'ai une souris blanche.

Home Life

Pages 10–11 Personal Information and Family
Test Yourself Answers
1. la souris – it is feminine
2. ma mère, mon poisson rouge, mes chats
3. J'ai deux chiens, trois chevaux et cinq oiseaux.
4. My cousin is an only child.

Stretch Yourself Answers
1. Mon ami(e) a une sœur qui a cinq ans.
2. J'ai un chat qui est noir et blanc.

Pages 12–13 Describing Yourself and Others
Test Yourself Answers
1. Ma mère a 37 ans et elle a les cheveux longs.
2. Ma sœur est petite et mince.
3. My cousin has hazel eyes.
4. My father is tall and thin.

Stretch Yourself Answers
1. Mon frère n'est pas aussi intelligent que ta sœur.
2. Je suis plus grand(e) que mon ami(e) mais je suis plus petit(e) que mon frère.

Pages 14–15 Character and Personality

Test Yourself Answers

1. Ma mère est sérieuse mais elle est sympa.
2. Ma sœur est ennuyeuse et paresseuse.
3. I am kind and funny.
4. My parents are strict and impatient.

Stretch Yourself Answers

1. La vieille dame achète une nouvelle voiture.
2. J'appelle mon oncle.

Pages 16–17 Relationships

Test Yourself Answers

1. Mes parents n'aiment pas mes vêtements.
2. Mon petit ami me rend triste.
3. You can rely on me.
4. My sister is single and she often argues with me.

Stretch Yourself Answers

1. Je ne me confie jamais à lui parce que nous ne nous entendons pas bien.
2. Vous vous disputez tout le temps, vous deux.

Pages 18–19 Relationships in the Future

Test Yourself Answers

1. Elle veut être riche et célèbre.
2. Je vais me marier à / avec un acteur.
3. I want to talk to your brother but I blush easily.
4. Sortir – which goes je sors, tu sors, il / elle sort, nous sortons, vous sortez, ils / elles sortent

Stretch Yourself Answers

1. Mon ami(e) a l'intention d'avoir une famille nombreuse.
2. J'espère aller à l'université parce que je pourrais devenir professeur.

Pages 20–21 House and Home

Test Yourself Answers

1. Au rez-de-chaussée, il y a un grand salon et une cuisine.
2. J'aime passer l'aspirateur mais je fais rarement le repassage.
3. My parents often work in the garden.
4. My brother's room is often in a mess.

Stretch Yourself Answers

1. Mon ami, qui est paresseux, a une sœur dont la chambre est très propre.
2. Elle a un frère dont la femme est allemande.

Pages 22–23 Talking About Your House

Test Yourself Answers

1. Dans ma chambre, il y a un grand lit et une armoire bleue.
2. Le jardin est derrière la maison qui est en face du magasin.
3. My house is near the shops.
4. In the lounge there is a sofa and two comfortable armchairs.

Stretch Yourself Answers

1. Je ne me lève jamais avant dix heures le week-end parce que j'aime faire la grasse matinée.
2. Je me douche et puis je m'habille.

Pages 24–25 Describing Your Local Area

Test Yourself Answers

1. Dans ma ville, il y a un grand centre commercial.
2. Tu dois / Vous devez visiter le vieux château.
3. I love going to the countryside because I like nature.
4. Thirty years ago, the town was calmer and less polluted.

Stretch Yourself Answers

1. Je finissais, je dormais, je disais, je buvais
2. La ville avait beaucoup de magasins et le centre-ville était animé.

Practice Questions Pages 26–27

(See the guidance on page 90.)

1. a) gentil
   b) paresseux
   c) généreuse
   d) sévère
2. a) in south-west France near Toulouse
   b) visit monuments, go for walks in the country, go shopping
   c) He doesn't like it; it is too calm; there is not enough to do; there is a lack of transport.

d) boring for young people; she lived there herself when younger.
e) in a big flat in London because he wants to improve his English

3. Example answers:
   a) Il y a quatre personnes dans ma famille: mon père, Vincent, qui est grand et beau, ma mère, Anne, qui est docteur, et ma sœur, Marion, qui est jolie et gentille.
   There are four people in my family: my father, Vincent, who is tall and handsome, my mother, Anne, who is a doctor, and my sister, Marion, who is pretty and kind.
   b) Ma maison est grande avec quatre chambres, trois salles de bains et un beau jardin. Au rez-de-chaussée, il y a un grand salon, une cuisine moderne et une salle à manger qui donne sur le jardin.
   My house is large with four bedrooms, three bathrooms and a beautiful garden. Downstairs, there is a large living-room, a modern kitchen and a dining room which overlooks the garden.
   c) Dans ma région, on peut faire du shopping au centre commercial. Il y a aussi beaucoup de musées et monuments pour les touristes.
   In my area, you can go shopping in the shopping centre. There are also lots of museums and monuments for tourists.
   d) J'aime ma région, mais quelquefois je la trouve un peu polluée et bruyante.
   I like my region but sometimes I find it a bit polluted and noisy.
   e) J'aime mieux la campagne parce que c'est propre et tranquille et on peut se relaxer dans le calme.
   I prefer the countryside because it is clean and quiet and you can relax in the calm.
   f) À l'avenir, je rêve d'habiter au bord de la mer en Espagne parce qu'il y fait chaud et j'adore la cuisine espagnole. J'aime aussi bronzer.
   In the future, I dream of living by the sea in Spain because it is hot and I love Spanish food. I also like sunbathing.

4. Example answer:
   Je m'appelle Sophie Laurent. Mon anniversaire, c'est le vingt-trois avril. J'ai les cheveux longs et bouclés. Je suis de taille moyenne. Je suis amusante, intelligente et sympa.

   J'ai un frère. Je n'ai pas de sœurs. Mon frère s'appelle Julien. Il a quinze ans. Il est assez grand. Il a les cheveux longs et raides et les yeux noisette. Il aime le sport mais il n'aime pas la musique. Il est intelligent, mais un peu égoïste. Ma meilleure amie s'appelle Claire. Elle est marrante et intelligente. Je m'entends bien avec les autres parce que je suis ouverte et sociable.

   J'habite dans l'est de la France. J'adore ma région parce qu'il y a beaucoup à faire, et c'est aussi calme et joli.

   Plus tard, j'ai l'intention de visiter l'Australie parce que je voudrais voir des kangourous.

   Je vais aller à l'université parce que je veux devenir dentiste.
   My name is Sophie Laurent. My birthday is the 23rd of April. I have long, curly hair. I'm of medium height. I'm funny, clever and nice.
   I have one brother and no sisters. My brother is called Julien. He is 15. He is quite tall. He has long, straight hair and hazel eyes. He likes sport but not music. He is clever but a bit selfish. My best friend is called Claire. She is funny and intelligent. I get on well with others because I'm open and sociable.
   I live in the east of France. I love my region because there is lots to do and it is calm and pretty.
   Later, I intend to visit Australia, because I'd like to see kangaroos.
   I'm going to go to university because I want to become a dentist.

School and Work

Pages 28–29 School and School Subjects

Test Yourself Answers

1. Je suis fort en français mais je suis faible en anglais.
2. Les bâtiments sont assez modernes.
3. I love maths because the teacher is kind.
4. I don't like music because the teacher is strict.

Stretch Yourself Answers

1. Je déteste mon prof, je le trouve ennuyeux et il ne me remarque pas.
2. Nous aimons l'histoire parce que nous la trouvons utile.

Pages 30–31 School Rules and Uniform

Test Yourself Answers

1. Il faut travailler dur et être attentif en classe.
2. Je suis pour l'uniforme parce que c'est pratique.
3. I am against school uniform because I do not like the colour.
4. I learn Spanish and it's easy.

Stretch Yourself Answers

1. À l'école primaire je ne portais pas d'uniforme mais je porte une cravate depuis trois ans à mon école secondaire.
2. J'ai joué au tennis pendant trois ans mais maintenant je ne l'aime pas.

Pages 32–33 School Life
Test Yourself Answers

1. My parents don't understand me. I find them too strict
2. In my school, the extra-curricular activities are excellent.
3. Mon ami parle trop en classe.
4. Nous travaillons tout le temps.

Stretch Yourself Answers

1. Je lui ai dit de faire ses devoirs mais il ne m'écoute pas.
2. J'aime mes professeurs. Je leur parle souvent.

Pages 34–35 Part-time Work and Pocket Money
Test Yourself Answers

1. I work 10 hours per / a week.
2. He doesn't like looking after his little brother.
3. Je gagne cinq livres de l'heure.
4. Elle veut trouver un travail.

Stretch Yourself Answers

1. Il continue à travailler et il refuse d'arrêter.
2. J'aide ma sœur à livrer les journaux.

Pages 36–37 Work Experience
Test Yourself Answers

1. I worked in a big office.
2. I found the work tiring and boring.
3. J'ai servi les clients – ils étaient très sympas.
4. Je ne veux pas travailler dans un magasin à l'avenir.

Stretch Yourself Answers

1. Mon patron m'a parlé après le déjeuner.
2. Les tables ne sont pas sales. Je les ai nettoyées hier.

Pages 38–39 Future Employment Plans
Test Yourself Answers

1. I want to become an engineer in later life.
2. He'll go to university.
3. L'année prochaine, je veux quitter l'école.
4. Ils travailleront dans un bureau.

Stretch Yourself Answers

1. Quand je me marierai, je travaillerai à l'étranger.
2. Quand je quitterai l'école, je trouverai un bon emploi.

Practice Questions Pages 40–41
(See the guidance on page 90.)

1. A l'anglais
   B les maths
   C les sciences
   D la musique
   E l'EPS
   F l'informatique / TIC
   G l'histoire
   H le dessin
2. a) Abdul
   b) Carole
   c) Églantine
   d) Églantine
   e) Flora
   f) Abdul
   g) Carole
   h) Flora
3. Example answers:
   a) L'école est assez moderne. Il y a une nouvelle bibliothèque, un centre sportif et un gymnase. Les cours commencent à neuf heures moins le quart et finissent à trois heures et demie. L'uniforme scolaire est bleu marine et on porte un blazer.
   The school is quite modern. There is a new library, a sports centre and a gym. Lessons start at 8.45 and end at 3.30. The uniform is navy blue and we wear a blazer.
   b) J'aime beaucoup le dessin parce que le prof est sympa et j'aime aussi l'histoire parce que c'est utile. En revanche, je n'aime pas du tout les sciences parce que je les trouve trop difficiles.

I like art a lot because the teacher is nice and I also like history because it's useful. On the other hand, I don't like science at all because I find it difficult.

   c) Il y a trop de règles. Les élèves pourraient porter des jeans. On aurait le droit de porter des bijoux. Je voudrais faire construire une nouvelle piscine.
   There are too many rules. Pupils could wear jeans. They would be allowed to wear jewellery. I would like to have a new swimming pool built.
4. Example answer:
   Après l'école, je veux devenir médecin parce que j'ai toujours voulu aider les autres. Le problème, c'est que j'ai peur du sang mais je suis forte en sciences et je rêve de gagner beaucoup d'argent.

   Je sais que je dois aller à l'université et donc j'ai besoin de très bons résultats à mes examens. La formation est longue mais je veux vraiment réussir.

   Je crois que j'irai en Afrique pour soigner des enfants malades. Ensuite, je reviendrai en Grande-Bretagne et je commencerai ma carrière.
   After school, I want to become a doctor because I have always wanted to help others. The problem is that I am frightened of blood but I am good at science and I dream of earning lots of money.

   I know that I must go to university and so I need very good results in my exams. The training is long but I really want to succeed.

   I think I will go to Africa to look after sick children. Afterwards, I will come back to Britain and I will start my career.

Lifestyle

Pages 42–43 Leisure Activities
Test Yourself Answers

1. I went out with my friends.
2. They love musicals.
3. J'ai vu le film samedi dernier.
4. Ils sont allés / Elles sont allées au concert hier soir.

Stretch Yourself Answers

1. Mon ami(e) venait de sortir quand je lui ai téléphoné.
2. Je n'aime pas les films. Ils deviennent ennuyeux.

Pages 44–45 More Leisure Activities
Test Yourself Answers

1. Do you feel like eating at my house?
2. She's just started learning to play the drums.
3. Tu veux faire une promenade?
4. Non, merci. Je dois me laver les cheveux.

Stretch Yourself Answers

1. J'ai trouvé un stylo. Elle dit que c'est le sien mais je pense que c'est le tien.
2. C'est à qui, cette flûte? C'est la mienne.

Pages 46–47 Shopping
Test Yourself Answers

1. This lift isn't working.
2. This supermarket is modern but very expensive.
3. Ce nouveau magasin est fermé le dimanche.
4. Je cherche une offre spéciale.

Stretch Yourself Answers

1. Ce porte-monnaie est joli mais ce portefeuille est moins cher.
2. Ces magasins-ci sont bons mais ces magasins-là sont moins chers.

Pages 48–49 Fashion
Test Yourself Answers

1. This shirt is too big.
2. These trousers are not too expensive.
3. Je cherche un tee-shirt long en coton.
4. Je porte des chaussures noires en cuir.

Stretch Yourself Answers

1. Voici des robes. Lesquelles préfères-tu? Celles-ci ou celles-là?
2. Quel pull est-ce que tu préfères? Celui-ci ou celui-là?

Pages 50–51 New Technology and the Media
Test Yourself Answers

1. There's too much advertising on TV.
2. Text messages are free for me.
3. Je joue aux jeux sur mon ordinateur.
4. Mon nouvel ordinateur est beaucoup plus rapide.

Stretch Yourself Answers
1. Les portables sont dangereux, ce qui est inquiétant.
2. Il passe beaucoup de temps sur l'ordinateur, ce qui est ennuyeux.

Pages 52–53 Events and Celebrations
Test Yourself Answers
1. He lit the candles.
2. She got a lot of presents.
3. J'ai mangé trop de chocolats à Pâques.
4. J'adore manger des crêpes.

Stretch Yourself Answers
1. Je ne me suis pas amusé parce que je me suis disputé avec ma petite amie.
2. Les garçons se sont couchés tard mais ils se sont amusés.

Pages 54–55 Sport and Exercise
Test Yourself Answers
1. I don't play rugby. It's violent.
2. They lost the match.
3. J'écoute de la musique en faisant du jogging.
4. Il adore jouer au tennis dans le parc.

Stretch Yourself Answers
1. J'étais sur le point de te téléphoner quand tu es arrivé.
2. Il est en train de faire ses devoirs.

Pages 56–57 A Healthy Lifestyle
Test Yourself Answers
1. I don't play rugby. It's not fun.
2. He has toothache and a temperature.
3. Je me couche tôt et je fais beaucoup d'exercice.
4. Il mange trop. Il a toujours faim.

Stretch Yourself Answers
1. Mon amie ne m'écoute jamais plus et personne ne peut la persuader de changer.
2. Il ne boit qu'une fois par semaine.

Pages 58–59 Smoking, Drugs and Alcohol
Test Yourself Answers
1. He smokes about 10 cigarettes a day.
2. She drinks too often; it's bad for the liver.
3. Les jeunes pensent qu'il est cool de fumer.
4. L'héroïne est une drogue dangereuse.

Stretch Yourself Answers
1. aille, puisse, fasse
2. Il fume bien que ce soit dangereux.

Pages 60–61 Food and Drink
Test Yourself Answers
1. You must eat lots of vegetables.
2. I don't like red meat. It's too fatty.
3. J'essaie de manger équilibré.
4. Elle ne mange jamais de viande rouge.

Stretch Yourself Answers
1. Le lait est bon pour la santé. J'en bois tous les jours.
2. J'aime les fruits. J'en mange tous les matins.

Practice Questions Pages 62–63
(See the guidance on page 90.)
1. a) Richard
   b) Pascal
   c) Céline
   d) Élodie
   e) Céline
   f) Céline
2. a) Cereal and hot chocolate
   b) She goes home and eats with her mum and sister.
   c) She never has it.
   d) She eats salad or yoghurt but not meat or fish.
   e) 7 a.m. in the kitchen
   f) He doesn't eat much and it's at about 8 p.m.
3. Example answers:
   a) and b) Le week-end dernier, j'ai fait du shopping au centre commercial près de chez moi. Je voulais acheter un cadeau pour l'anniversaire de mon ami.

Last weekend I shopped at the shopping centre near where I live. I wanted to buy a present for my friend's birthday.

c) and d) D'abord, je suis allée aux magasins de vêtements. J'ai vu une jolie robe noire. Je n'ai pas pu résister et j'ai acheté la robe. J'ai mangé un sandwich et j'ai bu un café. Ensuite, j'ai acheté un DVD pour mon ami.
First, I went to the clothes shops. I saw a pretty black dress. I couldn't resist and I bought the dress. I ate a sandwich and drank a coffee. Afterwards I bought a DVD for my friend.

e) and f) Je me suis bien amusée mais il y avait beaucoup de monde au centre commercial. La prochaine fois je vais y aller en semaine.
I had a good time but there were a lot of people in the shopping centre and next time I will go during the week.

4. Example answer:
Je suis en assez bonne forme parce que je fais du sport régulièrement. Le mardi, je vais à la piscine où je fais de la natation. Samedi dernier, je suis allé au gymnase pour faire de la musculation. C'était amusant mais fatigant.

   J'essaie de manger équilibré. J'aime les fruits et les légumes et il faut en manger cinq portions par jour. J'évite le chocolat et les bonbons parce qu'il y a trop de sucre dedans.

   À l'avenir, je ne vais jamais fumer parce que c'est trop dangereux et je vais boire de l'alcool avec modération.

   Je veux continuer à faire du sport et je vais éviter de manger trop de sucre, de graisse et de sel. Je voudrais vivre longtemps!
I'm in quite good shape because I do sport regularly. On Tuesdays I go to the pool where I swim. Last Saturday I went to the gym to do some bodybuilding. It was fun but tiring.

   I try to eat a balanced diet. I like fruit and vegetables and you should eat five portions a day. I avoid chocolate and sweets because there is too much sugar in them.

   In the future, I'm never going to smoke because it is too dangerous and I'm going to drink alcohol in moderation.

   I want to carry on doing sport and I'm going to avoid eating too much sugar, fat and salt. I'd like to live a long time!

The Wider World

Pages 64–65 Travel
Test Yourself Answers
1. I like relaxing in the garden.
2. I don't like going to Spain. It's too far.
3. Je suis allé(e) au Portugal en vacances.
4. J'aime faire des sports d'hiver.

Stretch Yourself Answers
1. J'adore l'Italie. J'y vais en mai.
2. Le cinéma est cher mais nous y allons deux fois par mois.

Pages 66–67 Getting Around
Test Yourself Answers
1. Turn left at the lights.
2. I don't like travelling by car, it's tiring.
3. Je voudrais un aller-retour pour Nice.
4. Ma voiture est tombée en panne sur l'autoroute.

Stretch Yourself Answers
1. Ne regarde pas la télé. Faisons une promenade.
2. Prenez la correspondance à Bordeaux et n'oubliez pas de me téléphoner.

Pages 68–69 Holiday Activities
Test Yourself Answers
1. On holiday I just want to relax.
2. I sunbathed, and then I swam in the sea.
3. Je voudrais passer trois semaines en Espagne.
4. Mon ami adore faire du shopping mais j'aime visiter des monuments.

Stretch Yourself Answers
1. avant de manger, après avoir bu, avant de voir, après être tombé(e)
2. Après être arrivée à la plage, elle a nagé dans la mer avant de bronzer.

Pages 70–71 Accommodation
Test Yourself Answers
1. A single room with a bathroom.
2. I would like to stay two nights.
3. Les douches ne marchent pas.
4. À quelle heure est le déjeuner?

Stretch Yourself Answers

1. Je me suis cassé(e) la jambe quand j'ai heurté un arbre.
2. On m'a volé mon porte-monnaie dans le parking.

Pages 72–73 The Weather

Test Yourself Answers

1. It's foggy in the north west of France.
2. Suddenly it began to rain. Luckily, it was hot.
3. Le ciel est vraiment gris.
4. Il fera extrêmement froid la semaine prochaine.

Stretch Yourself Answers

1. Il neigeait quand j'ai quitté la maison.
2. Je bronzais quand il a commencé à pleuvoir.
   Il faisait si froid qu'elle a mis un pull-over.

Pages 74–75 Life in Other Countries

Test Yourself Answers

1. The traditional costume is pretty.
2. The local speciality is delicious.
3. Elle est partie sans lui.
4. Les filles portent des bijoux traditionnels.

Stretch Yourself Answers

1. Elle avait joué, elle était arrivée, elle avait bu.
2. Quand il est arrivé dans le village, le festival avait déjà commencé.

Pages 76–77 The Environment

Test Yourself Answers

1. My town is polluted because of traffic.
2. We must recycle glass and paper.
3. Je vais à l'école à pied.
4. Les élèves vont au collège en autobus.

Stretch Yourself Answers

1. Une lettre sera écrite par Maman.
   Une tarte a été faite par Sophie.
2. Dans ma ville, le papier est recyclé par tout le monde.

Pages 78–79 Global Issues

Test Yourself Answers

1. We must save pandas and tigers.
2. It is important to reduce global warming.
3. Je pense que l'énergie solaire est utile.
4. Il faut protéger la planète.

Stretch Yourself Answers

1. Si nous le voulions (on le voulait), nous pourrions (on pourrait) protéger des espèces menacées.
2. Si on ne faisait rien, beaucoup d'animaux seraient menacés d'extinction.

Pages 80–81 Social Issues

Test Yourself Answers

1. I want to protest against unemployment.
2. Do you want to take part in a demonstration against the war?
3. J'ai l'intention de faire du travail bénévole.
4. Il faut combattre la discrimination.

Stretch Yourself Answers

1. Ce serait une bonne idée si on pourrait utiliser plus d'énergies renouvelables.
2. Il faudrait / On devrait collecter de l'argent pour combattre la pauvreté.

Practice Questions Pages 82–83

(See the guidance on page 90.)

1. a) B b) E c) D d) F e) A f) C
2. a) The Alps to go skiing.
   b) One week
   c) By train
   d) It was long and tiring.
   e) In a youth hostel.
   f) Went to a bar / drank wine / danced
   g) Very cold and it snowed a lot.
3. Example answers:
   a) Au mois de juillet, je suis allée à un petit village au bord de la mer en Italie. Il y avait un petit restaurant, une église et un magasin. J'y suis allée en avion et on a loué une voiture pour aller à l'hôtel.
      In July, I went to a little village by the sea in Italy. There was a small restaurant, a church and a shop. I went there by plane and we hired a car to get to the hotel.
   b) On a logé dans un hôtel confortable et propre au centre du village. On a bronzé à la plage et on a fait des excursions dans la campagne.
      We stayed in a clean and comfortable hotel in the centre of the village. We sunbathed on the beach and went on excursions in the country.
   c) Les vacances étaient très relaxantes. Je me suis bien amusé(e) parce qu'il a fait beau tout le temps et je me suis fait de nouveaux amis pendant mon séjour.
      The holiday was very relaxing. I had a good time because the weather was good all the time and I made some new friends during my stay.
   d) L'année prochaine, je voudrais aller aux États-Unis pour visiter la Floride. Je veux visiter les parcs d'attractions et loger dans une villa avec une piscine.
      Next year, I would like to go to America to visit Florida. I want to visit the theme parks and stay in a villa with a swimming pool.
4. Example answer:
   Dans ma ville, il y a trop de voitures et donc l'air est très pollué. Les rues sont sales parce qu'il y a beaucoup de papiers.
   À l'avenir, on devrait créer une zone piétonne au centre-ville. En même temps, il faut développer les transports en commun. Je veux encourager les gens à recycler le papier et le verre.
   Je rêve d'habiter à la campagne. Il n'y aura pas d'embouteillages ou de bruit et je voudrais habiter une petite ferme avec des animaux.
   J'ai l'intention de vivre à la campagne parce que la vie en ville est stressante et il y a trop de pollution à cause des voitures. La campagne est jolie et calme et on peut se relaxer dans la nature.
   In my town, there are too many cars and so the air is very polluted. The streets are dirty because there is a lot of litter.
   In the future, we should create a pedestrian zone in the town centre. At the same time we must develop public transport. I want to encourage people to recycle paper and glass.
   I dream of living in the country. There will not be any traffic jams or noise and I would like to live on a little farm with animals.
   I intend to live in the country because life in town is stressful and there is too much pollution because of cars. The countryside is pretty and calm and you can relax in nature.

Answers

Index